THE ULTIMATE WRECK SITE

BY ROY SMALLPAGE

UNDERWATER WORLD PUBLICATIONS

For my mother and father
Thanks for the mask, snorkel, and Worbarrow Bay

© Copyright 1994
by Underwater World Publications Ltd
55 High Street, Teddington, Middlesex TW11 8HA

Cover photograph: a ships' lantern on the *Hoyo Maru* (Lionel Pozzoli).
Inset: a gas mask, shoe and ammunition on the *Fujikawa Maru* (Roy Smallpage).

Book produced by DIVER Magazine
and printed by Emirates Printing Press,
PO Box 5106, Airport Road, Dubai, UAE.

ISBN: 0 946020 22 1

Also published by Underwater World:
Dive Kent by Kendall McDonald
Dive Sussex by Kendall McDonald
Dive Wight & Hampshire by Kendall McDonald and Martin Pritchard
Dive Dorset by John & Vicki Hinchcliffe
Dive South Devon by Kendall McDonald and Derek Cockbill
Dive South Cornwall by Richard Larn
Dive Isle of Man by Maura Mitchell and Ben Hextall
Dive West Scotland by Gordon Ridley
Dive North-west Scotland by Gordon Ridley
Dive Scotland – The Northern Isles and East Coast by Gordon Ridley
Dive North East by Dave Shaw and Barry Winfield
Dive Yorkshire by Arthur Godfrey and Peter Lassey

CONTENTS

FOREWORD

MANY years ago now, I was enjoying what I knew would be the first of many trips to Truk Lagoon. Spurred on by a legend of the superlative wreck diving inside the third largest coral reef in the world, I had left Britain with no information on the accommodation or diving facilities available there. I still remember landing at Moen with little more than my demand valve, mask, and underwater camera, and a vague hope that someone somewhere on the islands might be able to take me diving. Such uncertainty is not to be recommended. That is why I have written this book.

Entries in the wrecks section of the book are in alphabetical order, and include a summary of each ship's size and type, details about the wreck (depth, attitude etc), a brief account of its history, and a synopsis of what it has to offer the diver. A line drawing accompanies each entry to assist in identification. Wrecks are usually described bow to stern (proceeding from Number 1 hold to Number 4 or 5 where cargo areas are involved). Each paragraph starts with the area of the ship it deals with, to make life easier for the diver who only wants to visit part of a wreck.

I should like to thank the publisher for letting himself be convinced that more and more divers will want to travel to Truk Lagoon. I should also like to thank Martyn "Flug" Underdown for his assistance on the wreck location map, and researcher Bill Greenslade for helping me in the often tedious work of identifying military artefacts from the many slides. I should also like to thank the divers, guides, researchers, and production staff who have helped.

The author and publisher would be grateful for new information which adds to that provided here.

ROY SMALLPAGE

Opposite: a diver examines one of the many vehicles lost when Japanese vessels were sunk by American planes in 1944.

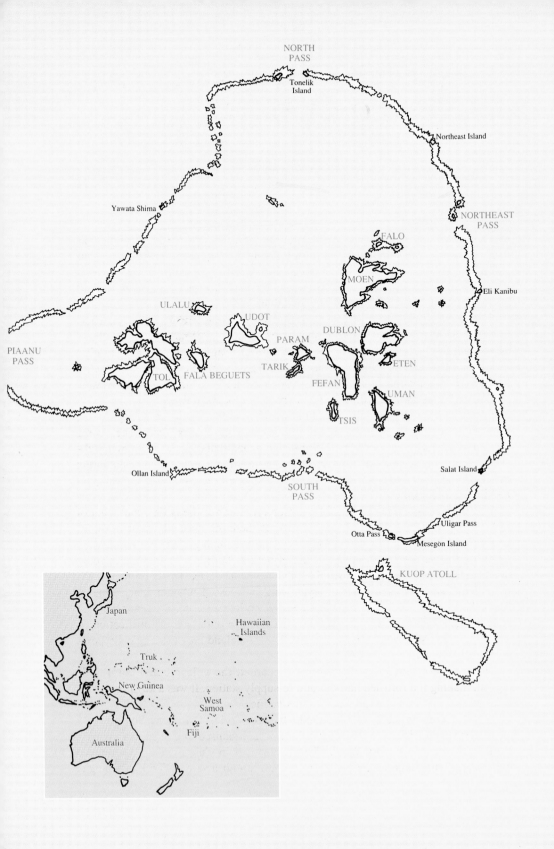

NORTH
PASS

Tonelik
Island

Northeast Island

Yawata Shima

NORTHEAST
PASS

Eli Kanibu

FALO

MOEN

ULALU

UDOT

PIAANU
PASS

PARAM

DUBLON

TARIK

ETEN

TOL

FALA BEGUETS

FEFAN

UMAN

TSIS

Salat Island

Ollan Island

SOUTH
PASS

Uligar Pass

Otta Pass

Mesegon Island

KUOP ATOLL

Japan

Hawaiian
Islands

Truk

New Guinea

West
Samoa

Fiji

Australia

TRUK IN THE SECOND WORLD WAR

T HE standard of diving in the Pacific is renowned, and one of its atolls contributes to this reputation by offering diving that has become legendary. Truk Lagoon is part of every diver's vocabulary, as well as some form of measuring stick for the rest of the world's diving. If divers have not actually been there themselves, they usually know of its reputation.

Situated just over seven degrees north of the equator, Truk Lagoon lies about 1,300 nautical miles south-east of Japan, and about 1,000 miles north of Papua New Guinea. It has a land area of only 127 square kilometres (49 square miles) divided up between its 290 islets and islands. The 140 mile coral reef that creates Truk Lagoon is the third largest reef in the world, and was discovered by western explorers 241 years before they found the continent of Australia.

Over 1,000 divers from all around the world visit Truk each year. They do not, however, come to see one of the world's largest natural coral reefs. They come instead to visit the lagoon within. For it is the lagoon that contains numerous well-preserved and protected wrecks which are the result of many Allied raids during the Second World War. Nearly 70 wreck sites have been guarded from plunder, and girded in corals.

In 1914 the Japanese Imperial Navy, fighting then for the Allies, took control of the German territories in the Pacific. At Truk there followed a level of construction and immigration hitherto unknown to the archipelago. The Japanese were quick to realise the importance of such a natural harbour for the empire they intended to build in the Pacific. In 1919, the Versailles Peace Treaty of the League of Nations mandated the islands to Japan, with a proviso that "no military or naval bases shall be established, or fortifications erected in the territory". Contrary to the stipulations of this mandate, Japan embarked on a programme of fortification of Truk which transformed the islanders and their homeland into a strategically powerful battle station.

The Japanese armed forces zealously guarded the volcanic and coral-built lagoon, making it a fortified harbour and re-supply station. It was a key possession in an empire that was spreading across the Pacific.

The Japanese termed these mandated island territories "The Inner South Seas", and on November 15, 1939, the Fourth Fleet was organised to protect them during Japan's "Greater East Asia War". The Commander in Chief of the Fourth Fleet then made Truk Lagoon his headquarters. Although aware of Truk's strategic importance to Japan, the Allies knew very little about it; but because of its excellent natural defences, Truk gradually became known as the "Gibraltar of the Pacific".

During the early part of the Second World War, the Japanese executed their programme of expansion with well-documented ruthlessness and vigour. The Battle of the Coral Sea on May 4-8, 1942, became the start of a new era in which aircraft carriers dominated naval warfare. The American Lt James Doolittle reinforced this importance by leading a carrier-based raid on Tokyo itself on April 18, 1942. The Battle for the Coral Sea also confirmed US suspicions that Truk was a major harbour for the Japanese Navy.

Codes were important in the Pacific war, and in an operation named "Magic", the US government had cracked a minor Japanese code. The US radio monitoring station on Hawaii picked up the harbour master of Truk Lagoon, routinely radioing in this minor code, and thereby obtained the names of Japanese aircraft carriers and the times they left Truk harbour. This vital information was used by US forces in the Battle of the Coral Sea.

The harbour master obligingly continued his disciplined routine of radioing the arrivals and departures of ships at Truk. The deciphering of his reports was crucial in many ways. As well as the time and dates of ship movements, the navy personnel on Hawaii were also able to inform the US High Command about some of the air search patterns used by the planes on Truk. Armed with such information, the American Admiral Nimitz was subsequently able to reduce the risk of his huge carrier-based force being spotted before its attack on Truk in February 1944.

The fortification of the archipelago continued right up to the time of the attack. During the summer of 1941, Truk received a number of 5- and 6-inch guns that were promptly installed as shore batteries, together with four twin-mounted 12cm anti-aircraft guns. The defensive force of Truk in 1943 was composed only of naval landing parties numbering about 1,000 men. In November 1943, with the front line inexorably moving west towards Japan, 300 officers and men of the HQ Company and Signal Corps arrived in Truk. On November 10 the Fourth Fleet transferred its headquarters from the flagship *Kashima,* to Truk. This involved about 250 personnel occupying the 4th Naval Supply building on Dublon.

In December 1943, Lt General Mugikura, Commanding Officer of the 31st Army and its 52nd Division, was posted to Truk. Inter-force co-operation on the islands, though, was minimal, with the Japanese Navy resenting the presence of the Army, and vice versa. Each force kept as separate as possible, with the result that communications between the two were sometimes very poor. On January 5, 1944, with the Allies advancing rapidly through the Pacific, 14,000 troops arrived to consolidate Truk against an invasion that never took place. One battalion of soldiers was kept on Moen, while two battalions were stationed on Tol. By February 1944, all the radar sets allocated for Truk had arrived, but in one of the most fundamental errors made, most of these remained unused, or were incorrectly installed. The Japanese expected an attack around February 21, 1944, but very few radars were made ready.

Searchlights were set up on Moen, Dublon, and Fefan. Suicide torpedo units, or Kaiten, were posted on Yanagi and Udot islands. These were placed with the intention of attacking any enemy shipping that entered or came close to the lagoon. Most of the passes into the lagoon were mined, denying access to all except the southern pass. This in turn was guarded by three guns and a Kaiten unit on Fanamu, to protect the Japanese thoroughfare.

The first attempt at a reconnaissance overflight came from the Royal Australian Air Force in January 1942. The resulting photographs of Truk confirmed a suspected build-up of Japanese forces for an invasion of Rabaul, 650 miles due south of the atoll. The Central War Room in Melbourne ordered an attack by six Catalinas, which were the only planes the RAAF had, capable of reaching Truk with a reasonable bomb load. Weather conditions were so bad over the islands however, that all planes had to return without dropping any ordnance. The Australian Chiefs of Staff then made a request that American Flying Fortresses based in Australia, make "even one strike" on Truk Lagoon. The request was denied. Another attempt on January 15, 1942, by six RAAF Catalinas from No 11 and 20 Squadrons, resulted in four of the aircraft making it to Truk, but only 16 bombs being dropped on the atoll. That same month, the Japanese Fourth Fleet sailed out of Truk and overran the Australian garrison in Rabaul.

By late January 1944, the 30th Base Force was set up in Truk to coordinate and command Japanese forces in the Western Carolines, and Palau. Allied victories were making Japanese forces retreat further and further. As a result of this, much of the Japanese fleet had retreated and gathered in Truk. On February 4, 1944, two US photo-reconnaissance planes made a 2,000-mile round trip from the Solomons to photograph the Japanese fleet at anchor in Truk. There was cloud cover over the islands, but several photographs were taken. The Dublon shore battery opened up on the aircraft, and it was not long before the other batteries of the lagoon, and even the ships' guns, were firing into the clouds.

This mission was enough to convince Admiral Koga that an attack by the Americans was imminent, and his Combined Fleet was in danger. At around 13.00 hrs local time, two carriers from the 6th Fleet anchorage, and three others from the Combined Fleet anchorage, moved out of Truk using the South Pass, because the North Pass was mined. The battleship *Yamato* and some cruisers left Truk soon after the carriers. Admiral Koga and his flagship the *Musashi* then retreated with four carriers, escorts and several of the fleet supply ships.

Once the reconnaissance photographs had been processed, the US forces could see that nearly all of the Japanese Combined Fleet had been at Truk. So the American High Command moved forward plans to attack the lagoon. This had originally been planned for April 15, 1944, but the prospect of destoying a greater part of the Japanese Fleet was too good to miss. Although the US submarine *Permit* reported that the warships *Nagato* and *Fuso* had left Truk and sailed west, the American admirals were not to know that only a few warships now remained in Truk. Two heavy cruisers were sighted leaving the lagoon on February 10, but more and more merchantmen were arriving, either from Japan, or retreating from

*Dauntless
divebombers peel
off to attack Ulalu
Island at the end of
April, 1944.*

places like Kavieng and Rabaul in New Britain, or the Marshall Islands. At this stage in the war, the front line was moving too fast for the Japanese. Supply ships setting off from Japan to reinforce outposts like the Solomons reached Truk to discover their destination had been overrun by the Allies. Bad weather had also hindered the unloading of supplies from many of the merchantmen in Truk, so scores of ships remained behind after the Japanese Combined Fleet left for Palau.

Admiral Nimitz ordered a strike force to sail on Truk, and put it under the command of Admiral Spruance. Planning now for a major engagement with the Japanese Combined Fleet, Admiral Spruance organised Task Force 50 into as mobile a group as he could manage. Selecting the fastest and best nine carriers, seven battleships, ten cruisers and 27 destroyers from the fleet that had just taken Kwajalein in the Marshalls, he organised them into three groups, and immediately moved off.

Apart from a few warships, most of the 80 or so vessels now at anchor in Truk

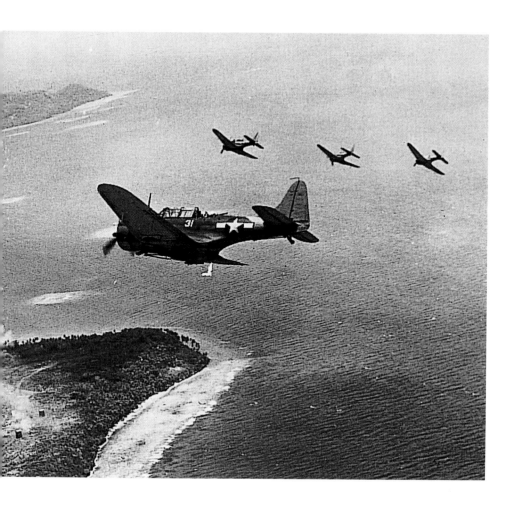

were armed merchantmen. Around February 14, the aircraft transport *Fujikawa Maru* started unloading much-needed planes onto the Eten airfield. Unloading was slow. Two previous ships had just offloaded about 30 aircraft only two days before. Hangar space was at a premium, and while the aircraft were lined up along the length of the big runway on Eten island, the mechanics and technicians were trying to re-assemble the fighters as soon as they were offloaded. The *Fujikawa Maru* managed to offload 11 aircraft from its aft holds.

On the morning of February 15, the Japanese Fleet Monitoring Unit intercepted a radio message from a US carrier pilot, and a number of aircraft were deployed in a search pattern around the lagoon. At 13.04 the radar operator of the light carrier *Belleau Wood* picked up a single aircraft. A combat air patrol of the same carrier was vectored onto it, and the US Hellcats duly shot down a single Japanese Betty bomber about 40 miles due west of Task Force 50. The action was over so quickly that the crew of the Betty were unable to get out any radio messages before they were killed. When two planes from the Japanese air patrol failed to return, the C-in-C of the Fourth Fleet, Vice Admiral Kobayashi, correctly ordered the highest state of readiness on Truk, but when after 12 hours the attack failed to come, he rescinded this alarm.

The 53 warships of Task Force 50 eventually sailed to a position 94 miles east-north-east of Dublon island on February 16 without being detected. The advantage of surprise was further enhanced by the attack beginning in the pre-dawn hours of the next day. Admiral Spruance knew that to stand any chance against the Japanese aircraft he must first gain air superiority. The initial objective then would be for the carriers to launch sufficient aircraft to destroy Truk's airfields and planes. At 04.40 on February 17 local time, 70 fighters and fighter bombers took off from five carriers. Coming in low to avoid the Japanese radar sets that were not yet working, the first wave flew over the two northerly passes, and after a 46-minute sweep around the lagoon, started straffing runs of the Japanese airfields – first the large airfield at the north end of Moen, then the seaplane base at its southern end, then on to Dublon, Eten and Param airfields. The attempt to knock out Truk, Operation Hailstone, was under way.

Having been stood down by their Commander, the Japanese pilots were in town, in bed, even on completely different islands from their fighter planes. Most of the air crew had been celebrating on Dublon, waiting for their compatriots returning from the recent action in Rabaul. The fighter pilots scrambled as fast as they could to get to their respective airfields, while the American pilots were straffing the Zero, Tojo, and Rufe fighters on the ground. Desperate to save as many of the planes as possible, officers were now ordering aircraft mechanics and technicians to take off and head north. Pilots arriving by boat or swimming across to Eten airfield were beaten up by their 2nd Commanding Officer.

Many of the local Trukese were not particularly disturbed by the loud explosions or gunfire in the lagoon, as the Japanese battleships such as the *Yamato* or the *Musashi* regularly fired their guns at targets or just for testing. Eye witness Kimiuo Aisek remembers having to be woken by his uncle, and thinking he was late for work with the Japanese. As soon as the Trukese realised this was the attack that had been expected, many of them took to the caves in the hills for cover.

Japanese planes were being shot down at a remarkable rate. On Eten airfield the congestion of recently offloaded planes, many of which were still not assembled, was so bad that attacking pilots saw Japanese fighters lined up wing-tip to wing-tip. Many aircraft were shot up as they taxied along the runway, or just after they had taken off. The sky was soon filled with hundreds of fighters, and numerous dog fights broke out. One pilot, Hamilton "One-Slug" McWhorter, remarked that "they fought as though they were in a daze". The 12 planes from the carrier USS *Enterprise* claimed 17 kills and five damaged. Meanwhile the 12 fighters from the carrier USS *Yorktown* were straffing Eten airfield, to keep its fighters from taking off and joining the fray. These pilots claimed nine Zero fighters, four Tojos, three Betty bombers, and five other assorted aircraft. With the fully fuelled Japanese planes crashing into other aircraft parked on the runway or apron, many fires soon spread across the airfields.

The 23 Grumman Hellcats from the carrier USS *Bunker Hill* were given orders to patrol the upper air space of between 20-25,000 feet. During this first sweep the flight encountered 15 Zeros and one Hamp. The Hamp was a confirmed kill, and the flight saw one of the Zeros falling towards the sea in flames, so it was listed as a probable.

The Japanese anti-aircraft fire was not radar controlled, so it could only put up a barrage as best it could. The crew of the large 6in gun on Dublon, having been told to expect an attack around February 21, had only just dismantled it for cleaning, so it remained silent throughout the attack. The officer in charge of this installation was subsequently executed.

According to Rear Admiral Michio Sumikawa, Chief of Staff of the Fourth Fleet, there were 365 aircraft in Truk at the time of the attack including twin-engined fighter-bombers from Germany. A hundred and twenty five aircraft from Operational Wings were destroyed on the ground, along with a further 110 from the Air Arsenal.

Quarter-ton bombs with time delay fuses were dropped on Param airfield, and

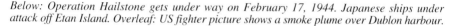

Below: Operation Hailstone gets under way on February 17, 1944. Japanese ships under attack off Etan Island. Overleaf: US fighter picture shows a smoke plume over Dublon harbour.

*Right: a Japanese
torpedo bomber
flies through a hail
of anti-aircraft fire
towards the USS
Yorktown during
the attack on Truk.*

when, days later, these bombs were collected by Japanese personnel, they started exploding at intervals. Many Japanese ground crew lost their lives, and the huge explosions could even be felt by people on Dublon and Moen islands.

The Japanese cruiser *Katori*, and the two destroyers *Nowake* and *Maikaze* managed to escape Truk via the North Pass, early on the morning of this first attack. Many Japanese personnel and civilians were also hastily put onto the *Akagi Maru*, a 7,398-ton six-hold freighter. This vessel also attempted to escape with the warships, but was attacked throughout the morning of February 17, and subsequently reported missing, presumed sunk, in its previously reported position 15 miles north-east of the North Pass.

Fighters from the USS *Yorktown* claimed a further 11 kills, including a Zero fighter that cartwheeled into a row of parked torpedo bombers. The Zero destroyed three of the parked planes, and hit a Betty bomber before coming to rest. Eight Grumman Hellcats reportedly destroyed three Mavis, and two Emily seaplanes on the ramps of the Dublon seaplane base. The 11 fighters of the USS *Essex*, claimed

21 Japanese planes shot down, with another probable. These fighters then went on to attack the airfield at Param, and the seaplane base at the south end of Moen. Here again, the Grumman Hellcats of the *Essex* claimed more kills – 15 aircraft destroyed on the ground at Param, and 12 float planes destroyed at the Moen seaplane base. During all this, the *Essex* flight lost only one fighter.

As the Grumman Hellcats from the *Intrepid* were attacking Moen's largest airfield in the north, they were themselves attacked by Japanese fighters. The American planes out-manoeuvred their enemy, and in the ensuing dogfight reportedly destroyed 11 of the Japanese fighters while sustaining no losses themselves. The Hellcats then went on to destroy a further 24 planes on the ground at Moen airfield. Executive Officer Lt G.C. Bullard, having completed 12 straffing runs of the airfield, retired to his flight's rendezvous point in the north. He spotted the light cruiser *Katori*, and led an attack on it. His plane was hit and downed, but he was seen to be alive just west of the North Pass. Subsequent flights report seeing his name in rocks and pebbles on the tiny Alanenkobwe island, and seeing him waving. He was, however, captured by some Japanese soldiers guarding the North Pass.

From 04.40 to 18.00 the task force launched nine waves of attacking planes. By 18.00 on February 18 there were only one Japanese fighter and four other aircraft reported to be left. Admiral Spruance now knew he had missed the Combined Fleet, but he had achieved air superiority, and was now able to concentrate on destroying the many ships that remained in the lagoon. Because of the minefields, shore batteries, and one-man suicide torpedo units, the US ships stood off, and it remained a solely aerial operation. Aircraft from the carriers *Belleau Wood*, *Cabot*, and *Monterey*, were largely kept in reserve to protect the task force in the event of any naval or air attack. A mixture of dive bombers and torpedo bombers would be protected by fighter escorts on attacks that went on throughout February 17 and 18. With no sign of any carriers, battleships, or many cruisers, target priority was given to submarines, oil tankers, fleet auxiliaries, and destroyers.

Despite missing the hoped-for engagement with the Japanese Imperial Fleet, the nine attack waves of Operation Hailstone were a complete success for the US forces. Forty-five Japanese ships (a total of over 220,000 tons) were sunk – a two-day record for the entire war. As well as these sinkings, a further 27 ships were damaged, and somewhere between 250 and 275 Japanese planes were destroyed. The submarine supply facilities and servicing stations were destroyed, the seaplane base on Moen was put out of action, 90 per cent of the atoll's fuel supply was set on fire, and all other airfields and installations were damaged.

US losses amounted to 12 Grumman Hellcats, 7 Grumman Avengers, and 6 Douglass Dauntless dive bombers. Twenty-nine aircrew were reported missing in action, and 11 sailors were killed when the carrier *Intrepid* was hit by a Japanese torpedo strike on the night between raids.

In Truk Lagoon itself, eyewitnesses remember only the smoke from scores of fires, as well as hundreds of bloated bodies washed up on the island shores along with wooden cargo crates and oil drums. The death toll in Truk is not known for certain, but Kimiuo Aisek, of the Blue Lagoon Dive Shop, remembers seeing 500-600 bodies being put into mass graves on the island of Dublon. The death toll continued to rise as the quarter-ton bombs armed with time-delay fuses exploded at odd intervals after the attack.

An official Japanese communique on the attack on Truk was issued on February 21, 1944. It read:

"On 17 & 18 February, 1944, Truk was attacked by an American task force operating in the area. The Imperial Army and Navy have fought excellently and repulsed successfully the attacks. The enemy lost two cruisers, and possibly one battleship. One large carrier was sunk, and an army ship destroyed. During the operation, 54 enemy aircraft were shot down. Our own losses are two cruisers, three destroyers, 13 transport ships, and 120 aircraft. Small damage was sustained on the islands."

The Japanese Army units on Truk blamed the Navy for not stopping the US task force further out to sea, and also demanded to know what the pilots were

Keeping score! Men of the Fighting Squadron Nine update their tally of kills aboard the USS Essex. Their total after the raid on Truk was 106 Japanese planes and six Vichy French.

doing on Dublon instead of at their alloted stations. The reinforcing of Truk, though, continued after Operation Hailstone, with over 30,000 troops on station by the end of March. By mid-April, all construction work on the defences was complete, and the radar units that were inoperative during Operation Hailstone were on line. For this reason, subsequent Allied attacks after Hailstone were not as effective. Not only had lessons been learned, but advance warning was sufficient to get most equipment under cover, and sufficient fighters in the air.

The list of Japanese ships sunk during Operation Hailstone reads as follows:

Aikoku Maru	passenger-freighter.
Akagi Maru	passenger-freighter.
Amagisan Maru	passenger-freighter.
CH 24	No 13 Class sub chaser.
CH 29	No 28 Class sub chaser.
Fujikawa Maru	passenger-freighter.
Fujisan Maru	fleet oil tanker.
Fumizuki	Mutsuki Class destroyer.
Gosei Maru	freighter.
Gyoraitei 10	T 51 motor torpedo boat.
Hakushun Maru	passenger-freighter.
Hanakawa Maru	passenger-freighter.
Heian Maru	submarine tender.
Hoki Maru	passenger-freighter.
Hokuyo Maru	passenger-freighter.
Hoyo Maru	fleet oil tanker.
Katori	light cruiser.
Kensho Maru	passenger-freighter.
Kiyosumi Maru	passenger-freighter.
Maikaze	Kagero Class destroyer.
Matsutan Maru	passenger-freighter.
Momokawa Maru	passenger-freighter.
Nagano Maru	passenger-freighter.
Naka	Sendai Class light cruiser.
Nippo Maru	passenger-freighter.
Oite	Kamikaze Class destroyer.
Reiyo Maru	passenger-freighter.
Rio De Janeiro Maru	passenger-freighter.
San Francisco Maru	passenger-freighter.
Sankisan Maru	freighter.
Seiko Maru	passenger-freighter.
Shinkoko Maru	fleet oil tanker.
Shonan Maru No 15	sub-chaser.
Tachikaze	Minekaze Class destroyer.
Taiho Maru	freighter.
Taikichi Maru	freighter.
Tatsuha Maru	passenger-freighter.
Tonan Maru No 3	fleet oil tanker.
Unkai Maru No 6	freighter.
Yamagiri Maru	passenger-freighter.
Yubae Maru	freighter.
Zukai Maru	freighter.

With the increasing number of US held territories such as Eniwetok, north-east of Truk, and the Solomon islands to the south, it was considered necessary to ensure that the Japanese in Truk were prevented from getting their aircraft out to bomb Allied forces. Admiral Nimitz therefore planned another carrier-based attack on April 29-30. With many of the Japanese shipping routes now closed off due to Allied victories in the Pacific, and due to Truk almost being in the front line, it was no longer used as a major harbour. Therefore fewer ships were sunk in these raids. The US forces claimed to have destroyed 60 aircraft on the ground, and to have shot down a further 63 in dog fights over Truk, while losing 35 of their own planes. Ships sunk in this attack include the freighter *Dai Na Hino Maru No2* (the Gun High wreck), the Minelayer *Minsei Maru*, the sub-chaser *No38*, and the sub-chaser *Sapporo Maru*, which was damaged by bombs and later sank as a result on May 4. As well as these four ships, other smaller tugs, harbour vessels, barges and sampans were seen to have been destroyed. The submarine *I-174* was also sunk by depth charges from the destroyer *Stephen Potter*.

On May 1, 1944, the Japanese 4th Base Force Headquarters on Truk demobilised. Later the same month 71 aircraft (59 of which were fighters), were moved from Truk to Guam and Yap. The importance of Truk diminished, as the 290 islands of the lagoon were gradually cut off from Japan.

It's all over bar the shouting. Lt Col Cyril Emrich, of the US Marine Corps, reads Proclamation No 1 to Japanese and natives on Truk at the end of hostilities.

ULALU

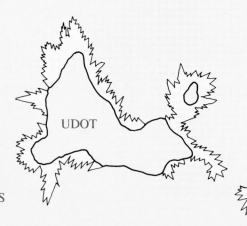

38

UDOT

1

PARAM

FALA BEGUETS

47

39

TARIK

THE WRECK SITES OF TRUK LAGOON

1...SHINKOKU MARU	25...KIKUKAWA MARU
2...YAMAGIRI MARU	26...HOKI MARU
3...I-169 SHINOHARA	27...FUJIKAWA MARU
4...TONAN MARU No 3	28...UNKAI MARU No 6
5...HEIAN MARU	29...GOSEI MARU
6...TAIKICHI MARU	30...RIO DE JANEIRO MARU
7...KENSHO MARU	31...YUBAE MARU
8...KIYOSUMI MARU	32...TAIHO MARU
9...SAPPORO MARU	33...THE LIGHTER
10...HOYO MARU	34...HINO MARU
11...EISEN No 761	35...HARBOUR BOAT
12...FUTAGAMI	36...SANKISAN MARU
13...SUSUKI	37...AMAGISAN MARU
14...FUJISAN MARU	38...FUMIZUKI
15...NIPPO MARU	39...HANAKAWA MARU
16...AIKOKU MARU	40...OITE
17...MOMOKAWA MARU	41...EMILY FLYING BOAT
18...REIYO MARU	42...BETTY BOMBER
19...NAGANO MARU	43...ZERO FIGHTER
20...SAN FRANCISCO MARU	44...KATE TORPEDO BOMBER
21...MATSUTAN MARU	45...JUDY DIVE BOMBER
22...SEIKO MARU	46...ZERO FIGHTER
23...HOKUYO MARU	47...ZERO FIGHTER
24...OJIMA	48...DUMPING GROUND

40
(NORTH PASS)

MOEN

BUSH

YANAGI

14

HERIT

2

3   4

5

15

6   7

8

9   10

11

12

13

48

DUBLON

16

17   18

19

20   21

22   23

FANAMU

41

44   45

43   46

ETEN

24

25

26

42

27

FEFAN

28

29

31

32

33
34
35
36
37

UMAN

30

TSIS

FALEAT

FANANAN

FANEU

16

NAME:	AIKOKU MARU.
TONNAGE:	10,437.
DIMENSIONS:	150m x 20m x 12.4m.
SHIP TYPE:	Passenger-Freighter.
SUNKEN ATTITUDE:	Upright on a fairly even keel.
DEPTH TO SEABED:	64m to 75m.
DEPTH TO WRECK:	40m (top of bridge remains); 49m (deck).
FEATURES OF NOTE:	Anti-aircraft guns on boat deck.
	Prominent stern gun. Human remains.

BUILT in 1939 in Okajima, by Tama Zosensho K.K. The *Aikoku Maru* had luxury accommodation for 48 first-class, 48 "special" third-class, and 304 "regular" third-class passengers. It was to have been used as a passenger/cargo liner on the Japan-Africa route by its owners Osaka Shosen K.K. Not having been completed until August 1941, she never came to fulfill her civilian role because the Japanese Navy requisitioned her. Her six cargo holds, along with her capability of accommodating 400 passengers, made her an important transport ship; so in recognition of this, the navy fitted eight 5.5in guns, four torpedo tubes, and two twin-barrelled anti-aircraft guns. The eight 5.5in weapons were later replaced by two 7.62cm type 88s in October, 1943. Having thus been converted to an armed merchant cruiser shortly after being built, she formed, along with her sister ship *Hokoku Maru* and the *Kiyosumi Maru*, the Special Cruiser Squadron 24, an integral part of the Combined Fleet. *Kiyosumi Maru* was to be sunk like *Aikoku Maru* in Operation Hailstone.

In conjunction with her sister ship, the *Aikoku Maru* was ordered on search and destroy missions in the Pacific. The *Aikoku Maru* received further alterations to assist her in this task. Cradles were fitted to carry two reconnaissance float planes. The two ships were responsible for the sinking or capture of a variety of Allied vessels before the *Hokoku Maru* was hit and sunk during an attack on a tanker on November 11, 1942. On July 16, 1943, the *Aikoku Maru* was spotted north of Truk Lagoon by the US submarine *Halibut*. A torpedo hit the *Aikoku Maru* causing 21 casualties and medium damage. After temporary repairs in Truk Lagoon, the ship then sailed on to Japan. In January 1944, the *Aikoku Maru* departed in a convoy on a secret mission. She was loaded with troops bound for the Marshall Islands, but by the time the ship was near, the Marshalls had been taken by US forces. Some of her passengers were off-loaded at Ponape, then the

Aikoku Maru sailed for Truk, arriving and anchoring on the evening of February 16, 1944, local time.

At about 08.15 on the morning of February 17, the *Aikoku Maru* was attacked by the fourth wave of fighter bombers taking part in Operation Hailstone. With the Japanese anti-aircraft gunners firing like mad on the boat deck, the hundreds of troops below decks were only able to listen to the battle that raged above their heads. Lt Briggs flew his Avenger bomber and two man crew low over the bow, dropping a 500lb bomb right into one of the forward holds. This caused an immediate secondary detonation of the cargo of ordnance being carried. There was a cataclysmic explosion, and the *Aikoku Maru* was gone. Gone too was Lt Briggs, his crew of two, and his Avenger bomber. She lies today, just as she was shortly after that explosion. The anti-aircraft guns remain as they were at the moment of impact, barrels in mid-recoil, with belts of ammunition still held in their breeches. The shattered bones of the hundreds of troops and crew lie strewn across the decks. The front half of the ship literally disappeared. It does not even exist as wreckage on the seabed. A search has been made for this half, but all that was found was a corner section of one cargo hold. Today the *Aikoku Maru* rests in a crater on the sea bed – a crater formed by the huge explosion that destroyed her.

DIVING INFORMATION

THE *Aikoku Maru* is upright with the forward part of the wreckage in 73m, and the stern in 64m. The vessel is intact from the huge smoke stack to the stern. Forward of the stack, the bridge and various deck levels beneath it lie collapsed, pointing down to the sea bed. It is as though the whole ship was cleaved cleanly in two. Nothing remains of either the bow, forecastle, or forward holds.

The midships superstructure is the forwardmost, and shallowest part of the *Aikoku Maru*. At 40m the upper boat deck is the shallowest part of the wreck. From this towers the funnel, which, having been protected from the blast by the bridge, remains intact. Aft of the stack, divers will find the engine room skylights, and quite surprisingly, some ventilation cowls. Bearing in mind the ferocity of the explosion that destroyed this vessel, it is a real surprise to find intact examples of not only the ventilator shafts, but also their cowls or air scoops. Behind the skylights, on the same upper deck, are the twin-barrelled 13.2mm port and starboard anti-aircraft guns. Ammunition can still be seen being fed into the breech of one of these guns. Both these heavy weapons are thickly caked in corals. Next, on the aftmost section of the boat deck is an equally large and coral-covered piece of machinery. This was part of the fire control and range-finding equipment for the ship's guns. Nothing remains of the lifeboats that give this deck its name.

Below the boat deck are the promenade, shelter, and maindeck. Due to the destruction of the bow section of the ship, the bridge and all decks below it have collapsed, and are pointing downwards. This makes entry to the lower decks difficult, not to say dangerous, here. The best way to gain entry to the lower decks is via the large two-metre-square glassless windows, or the doors on both the port and starboard sides of promenade deck. Access is also good at the aft end of promenade

deck. All wooden doors, glass windows, and most plywood partitions were blasted to bits in the explosion, and have since decomposed. The clarity of the water here, in combination with this destruction, and the large saloon-type windows (rather than portholes) make the *Aikoku Maru* much lighter inside than other Truk wrecks. However, there are many electric cables hanging in loops or otherwise sagging from the ceiling because their cable-ties or thin metal fastenings have rotted away. This makes it easy for the unwary diver to get his main cylinder valve or hoses caught in the resulting cobweb of copper and steel. Sensible finning, and use of a good torch, will help prevent this. There are plenty of large rooms without this hazard, and it is in these that the splintered remains of crew and troops can be found. So violent was the blast that it not only ripped doors off hinges, smashed all the windows, and buckled bulkheads, but it also apparently broke limbs like pencils. The bones of many of these limbs lie strewn across the decks here. The shock waves also blew most of the lighter artefacts towards the stern end of each cabin. Sinks stand incongruously alone, supported only by their plumbing, the wall partitions they were attached to having been blasted or rotted away.

Below the promenade deck is the shelter deck, or main deck, and it is at the aft end of this that the large galley can be found. A huge stove and heaps of crockery, mostly broken, but much of it intact, are the first things that you see. Taps, pipework, a broken sink, cooking utensils, and dozens of bottles can also be found.

Number 4 hold, just aft of the superstructure, is raised one deck higher than its two aft counterparts, and resembles a shaft with walls on all four sides. This is in marked contrast to the normal hold layout of 'tween decks below main deck to maximise floor space for cargo. The reason is that the 'tween decks had been altered to make accommodation for troops. Two levels of hatchcover beams have to be negotiated before a doorway is found at 55m, giving access to these labyrinthine quarters. As these quarters are below 50m, and reliably reported to be full of silt, divers are not advised to explore them using compressed air apparatus. It was in these quarters that many of the human remains were located by earlier diving expeditions. A vast quantity of bones still remain, although the Japanese authorities have since recovered many of the skulls to complete the proper Shinto burial rites for these men. Aft of Number 4 hold can be found a winch house, complete with electrical circuitry, two large motors and cargo winches.

Number 5 hold is one deck lower still, and like its forward counterpart is too deep for a sport diver using compressed air to explore. This hold is conventionally layed out with 'tween decks. There are reports of human remains having been found on the for'ard 'tween decks of this hold, although it is likely that these too have been recovered by the Japanese authorities.

Number 6 hold is smaller than the previous two, with a deckhouse aft of it. An 8cm type 88 gun is mounted on a gun platform above this deckhouse. As with the other deck guns in Truk Lagoon, this one is cloaked in corals. It points skywards over the port side of the ship, and, like the AA guns on the boat deck, is likely to have been manned and firing during the air attack. Also to be found around this deckhouse and covered walkway are fairleads, mooring bits, and a capstan.

Opposite: human remains.
Overleaf: a gun on the San Francisco Maru.

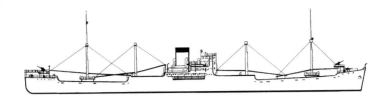

NAME:	AMAGISAN MARU.
TONNAGE:	7,620.
DIMENSIONS:	137m x 18.26m x 11.27m.
SHIP TYPE:	Passenger cargo.
SUNKEN ATTITUDE:	45 degree list to port. Sloping seabed.
DEPTH TO SEABED:	75m (at stern).
DEPTH TO WRECK:	30m (to bow gun).
FEATURES OF NOTE:	Road tanker on sea bed. Staff car in hold.

THE *Amagisan Maru* was built in 1933 by Mitsui Bussan Kaisha. She could accommodate 48 crew and seven passengers. The single screw, driven by her 1,230nhp diesel engine, could give her a maximum speed of almost 19 knots.

Like most ships of her class, the *Amagisan Maru* was requisitioned, and armed by the Japanese Navy for service in the Pacific. The Japanese harbour master at Truk made a radio transmission on February 14, 1944, to the effect that six ships had entered his jurisdiction. One of them was the *Amagisan Maru*. The captain anchored his vessel on the west side of Uman, and less than two days later the *Amagisan Maru* was torpedoed once or maybe twice during Operation Hailstone. The *Amagisan Maru* was reported sunk at 1300 hrs on February 16 US time, which was one day behind local time. It is not known how many casualties there were.

DIVING INFORMATION

THE *Amagisan Maru* lies on a very steep slope of the seabed, with a 45 degree list to port. Her stern lies in very deep water, but a good dive can be enjoyed around the bow, first three holds, and superstructure of this lesser known and lesser dived wreck of the lagoon.

As with most wrecks in Truk, it is generally custom and practice to lower the anchor/shot onto the shallowest portion of the wreck. This is a commonsense measure, giving divers the best choice of how deep they wish to go. On the deeper wrecks, it is of course preferable to end your dive on the shallower portion.

The bow is considerably shallower than the stern. The port anchor chain is out, and stretches over the seabed, and the starboard anchor is not properly stowed, so it is likely the crew were in the process of weighing anchor so that the ship could get under way. Aft of the deck rails, hawse pipes, and windlasses, there is the 3.7in gun, which is very picturesque. It is, like most of the deck guns here, covered in coral. It sits on a gun platform just over a metre above the forecastle deck.

Number 1 hold is basically empty, with the exception of several fuel oil drums. Moving further aft, there is the winch house, with two winches located on the roof. The derricks have collapsed and swung across the decks with the list of the boat. They now point to the wreck of a tanker lorry on the seabed. It is 41 metres here. With the exception of some of the bodywork, most of the lorry is intact.

Number 2 hold contains wooden planking, aircraft wings and other parts, as well as more fuel oil drums. Still moving towards the superstructure midships, in the same hold, there are the remains of a Japanese officer's staff car among the cargo of wood. At this depth there is very little coral growth, and apart from a big dent and a hole in the roof, the car is in quite a remarkable state of preservation. There is evidence all around here of the fierce fire that raged on board following the first torpedo hit.

Number 3 hold is slightly elevated above 1 and 2. It was this hold that the US torpedo hit on the starboard side. There is of course a sizeable hole below what was the water line. The evidence of a serious fire is all around the forward section of the ship, and doubtless this was where it started. The hold, therefore, is more devoid of artefacts than the others.

The superstructure rises three decks above main deck level. First is the mess deck, with plenty of crockery, and some cutlery. Most of this has of course fallen to the port side of the wreckage with the list of the ship on the seabed. A few pieces can still be found with the Mitsui owner's emblem. Above the mess deck on the port side can be found the large cabinet-sized ship's radio transmitters. Above this is the bridge. Still upright here are the helm, and ship's telegraph. Other pieces of navigational equipment have fallen to the port side. With its proximity to the torpedo hit and subsequent fire, it should come as no surprise that the wooden planking is charred.

Aft of the midships superstructure is the smoke stack, with its three rings denoting ownership by the Mitsui Line. Also visible here are the anti-aircraft gun platform (the gun has fallen off), the engine room skylights, and a few ventilators.

The part of the ship aft of the superstructure is too deep for exploration, but it is possible to swim along at mast height and view the damage on the starboard side at stern, made by the second torpedo that hit the *Amagisan Maru*.

NAME:	EISEN No 761.
TONNAGE:	300 (displacement).
DIMENSIONS:	34.4m x 6.7m x 3m.
SHIP TYPE:	Harbour tug.
SUNKEN ATTITUDE:	Upright.
DEPTH TO SEABED:	20m.
DEPTH TO WRECK:	12m to the bridge.
FEATURES OF NOTE:	Bridge area and Engine Room.

THIS tugboat would have had a complement of 7 men, and its coal-fired 1,200ihp engine would have been capable of 8 knots. Due to the ring of shallow coral reef that encircled Dublon, and the fact that Dublon had no wharf or pier for any ship to tie up to or unload onto, *Eisen No 761*, along with other tugs, was used to ferry barges of cargo from ships at anchor to the island.

DIVING INFORMATION
NOT far from Dublon island, opposite the wrecks of the Japanese landing craft on the west side of the island, this wreck is appreciably smaller than the other tug *Futagami*. Points of interest are: the searchlight on top of the navigation bridge, the bridge itself, with the two engine telegraphs, binnacle, compass, and speech tubes. Also the tiny galley, and the small engine room which can get very silty after a short while, so care should be taken during any exploration of this area. There is plenty of coral and sponge growth on this wreck.

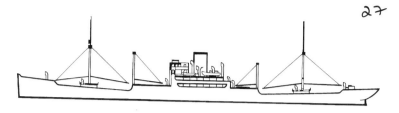

NAME:	FUJIKAWA MARU.
TONNAGE:	6,938.
DIMENSIONS:	133m x 17.83m x 10m.
SHIP TYPE:	Freighter.
SUNKEN ATTITUDE:	Upright on an even keel.
DEPTH TO SEABED:	34m.
DEPTH TO WRECK:	15m (superstructure).
FEATURES OF NOTE:	Fighters in hold 2. Bow and stern guns. Coral/marine life.

THE *Fujikawa Maru* was built in 1938 by Mitsubishi Heavy Industry for the Toyo Kaiun K.K. line. It was driven by a single screw, powered by a Mitsubishi-Sulzer diesel. With about 840nhp this meant a maximum speed of around 16 knots. She could carry a complement of 40 crew, plus four passengers.

For two years the ship was used first as a liner plying between Japan and the eastern seaboard of the United States, then a couple of months later as a passenger/cargo vessel sailing to South America and India. Requisitioned into military service on December 9, 1940, the ship was converted to carry aircraft for the 11th Air fleet in Indo-China. She was then armed with two old English Vickers Armstrong 6in guns. These had been taken from de-commissioned cruisers and were fixed to the bow and stern. As part of Air Flotilla 22, the *Fujikawa Maru* ferried planes to wherever they were needed. During late 1941 or early 1942, she started ferrying planes to the mandated islands.

The ship was spotted by a US submarine and subsequently hit by a torpedo on September 12, 1943, whilst sailing from Kwajalein in the Marshall Islands, to Truk. She made it to Truk four days later, where repairs were made. The ship also underwent a convertion from an aircraft ferry to a general transport. This was completed in January, 1944. The *Fujikawa,* though, continued carrying aircraft and aircraft parts, for, when she was sunk in Operation Hailstone, the vessel had just unloaded 30 Jill torpedo bombers onto Eten airfield. When a single torpedo hit the *Fujikawa Maru* just aft of the superstructure on the starboard side, she was still carrying four Zero fighters, and a host of aircraft parts.

DIVING INFORMATION
THE *Fujikawa Maru* is often one of the first wrecks in Truk Lagoon that divers see. Both its masts used to stand out of the water, until a combination of rotting

metalwork and the sheer weight of corals on one became too much, and it collapsed, scaring the wits out of a local fisherman. Today only one of the masts can still be seen poking out of the water.

The bow and forecastle are in a fine state of preservation. Aft of the capstan can be found the English Vickers Armstrong 6in gun. The maker's brass plate, located on the breech, can still be read, and gives the date of manufacture as 1899. It is protected by sloping armour on three sides. Despite coral growth, many of the workings can still be made out. There are several open boxes of ammunition behind the breech, lying on the raised gun platform. The gaps in these boxes, coupled with hastily-discarded spent shell cases that can still be found at the bottom of Number 1 hold, suggest this gun was not only manned but in action just before its sinking. The shallow depths here, and the fantastic corals that grow around the ship, let alone the foc'sle, make this a photogenic subject. Secured to the bulkhead on the starboard side of the foc'sle there is a spare anchor. There are two entrances into the foc'sle and an array of coiled hoses, cables, gasmasks, and some large shell cases.

Number 1 hold goes down to about 27m. This hold contains an odd assortment of military bric-a-brac and is reached by swimming down between the arched hatch beams. On the first 'tween deck, port side, there is a torpedo, with the blue painted bodywork largely intact. At the bottom of the hold there is an odd assortment of grey-clothed model 93-No2 Navy gas masks, clips of 6.5mm ammunition for the Japanese Arisaka infantry rifle, belts of machine gun ammunition, aircraft wheels, propeller blades, fighter-wing fuel tanks, pulley blocks, rolls of wire, hundreds of empty brass shell cases, and even an outboard motor. Most of the shell cases are a neatly stored reminder that at the moment of this ship's sinking Japan was suffering badly from a lack of raw materials, and these shells would almost certainly have been on their way back to the armaments factories for re-cycling. On top of this neatly stacked brass cargo can be found a haphazardly strewn number of smaller shell cases that probably came from the breech of the *Fujikawa's* bow gun. The chaotic nature of their stowage suggests the gun was in use before the ship's sinking. The 'tween decks at the aft end of this hold carry a cargo of fuel oil drums, some of which were empty but air-tight at the time of sinking, and were consequently crushed like paper cups.

Between Numbers 1 and 2 holds can be found the winch house for operating the cargo derricks. It is very silty, but inside there is an array of sailors' mess tins and gasmasks.

Number 2 hold is reached by swimming through two deck levels of hatch beams, and also goes down to about 27m, but the effort is well rewarded, for at the bottom of this hold can be found at least four Japanese fighters. The remnants of paint are covered by a patina of oxidisation and silt, but apart from this they are in remarkable condition. The fire on board the *Fujikawa* was reasonably short lived, for although all the fighters' gauges are smoke-blackened, they can still mostly be read. The control column (joystick), and other controls are all still moveable. With care it is even possible to climb into the cockpits of several of these aircraft. The pilot's seat in these planes was more comfortable than those of the Allies, because it was the custom for the Allied pilots to use their parachutes as cushions, so their seats had to be recessed to accommodate the parachutes. Japanese seats have no such recess, because their pilots did not wear parachutes. In this hold there are more fuel oil drums, empty beer bottles, and some aircraft bombs.

Number 3 hold is elevated one deck above the main deck and the previous two holds. There are two short flights of steps, one on the port and the other on the starboard going up to this deck. The hold is basically empty, with the exception of some fuel oil drums. There are two corridors, port and starboard, that travel underneath the ship's midship superstructure all the way to Number 4 hold. The various rooms leading off these passageways contain a lot of silt, so full exploration is difficult, but there are many beer and sake bottles to be found.

The superstructure midships rises four decks above shelter deck. Little now

Ammunition, a discarded leather shoe and a gas mask among the assortment of military bric-a-brac to be found in the holds of the Fujikawa Maru, one of Truk's most dived wrecks.

remains of the flying bridge, but there is a coral-covered twin-barrelled AA gun mounted nearby. The smoke stack is impressive, even though some of its outer metalwork has corroded through. There are some fabulous coral growths in and around it. The navigation bridge underneath contains an assortment of nautical paraphernalia such as deckhead lights, ship's compass, brass fittings and so on. The ship's telegraph and rudder stand have apparently fallen through the wooden decking to a position one or two decks below. There is a tangle of cables and wiring, and a general air of destruction here, but at around 15m there is plenty of available light. Going down one deck, along the port side, you will find the captain's quarters, his bathroom, which is in superb condition, and the officers' quarters. Entry and exit can also be made from holes rotted in the deck head or ceiling. It is also possible to see the ship's radio sets here. Most of the wooden partitioning has gone now, but the portholes and deck fittings remain. Descending again, the ship's galley can be found at the aft end of this deck. The galley contains a huge stove, bronze grinder, water heater, and crockery. Nearby can also be found a huge stack of "Dai Nippon" beer bottles in one room, and also on the port side, one of the ship's heads, with rows of urinals and hand basins in excellent condition. Venturing down to the engine room by way of the companionways and passages inboard, the metal gantries, steps, and catwalks lead down to six large cylinder heads, high pressure pipes, valves and smoke-stained guages.

Number 4 hold on the starboard side is where the torpedo hit. Here the ship's plating was split and ruptured, in the explosion. It is possible for a diver to swim through this hole. The hold is otherwise devoid of interesting features.

Number 5 hold is likewise void of interesting features, and more than likely contained some of the cargo of planes that were reportedly offloaded before the attack.

A winch house of similar design to that located on the foreship is situated between Numbers 5 and 6 holds.

Number 6 hold contains on its 'tween decks, literally thousands of "Dai Nippon" beer bottles. The amount is staggering. Further aft on the 'tween decks can also be found galley stores of rice kettles, traditional kettles, pans, mess tins, packaged chopsticks, plus assorted crockery, bottles and jars. Some of the crockery supports the anchor and rising sun emblem of the Japanese Navy, although these items are disappointingly vanishing into the goody bags of unscrupulous divers. Further down, at about 35m, there are crates of stores that have not yet been opened. At the aft end of this hold on one of the 'tween decks can be found a large compressor. Nearby, but much further in, can be found a bank of a dozen big CO_2 cylinders and high-pressure piping. These would have been used to fight fires. The valves and gauges are all intact, although the gauges are fire damaged.

The sterncastle can be entered by either of two doorways. The rooms inside are very dark and contain unopened boxes, and coils of various-sized rope. The deck gun is the same model as that on the bow, and is pointing forward over the starboard side. The ship's propeller is an impressive sight down at 36m, and sharks occasionally gather around this stern area.

Opposite: cockpit of a Japanese fighter in the Fujikawa Maru.

14

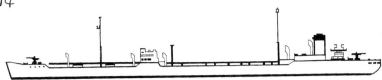

NAME:	FUJISAN MARU.
TONNAGE:	9,524.
DIMENSIONS:	156m x 19.81m x 11.28m.
SHIP TYPE:	Oil tanker.
SUNKEN ATTITUDE:	45 degree list to port.
DEPTH TO SEABED:	61m.
DEPTH TO WRECK:	37m (to bridge).
FEATURES OF NOTE:	The bridge area.

LAUNCHED on May 31, 1931, the *Fujisan Maru* was built by Harima Sanbashi Engineering for Lino Shoji Kisen Kaisha as a tanker. Unloaded, her single screw, powered by the 7,200hp MAN-Diesel engine, could drive the empty ship a maximum of 18.79 knots.

The vessel was first used to carry crude oil between Japan and the United States, but was later requisitioned by the Japanese Navy in 1941. The *Fujisan Maru* was involved in the successful Japanese invasion of the US Aleutian islands of Kiska and Attu in 1942. The ship was also used to carry a "deck cargo" of 1900 troops to reinforce the beleaguered Japanese-held New Guinea. Hit by a bomb from a US B-17 in December 1943, the *Fujisan Maru* was repaired and back in service weeks later. On February 17, 1944, the *Fujisan Maru* was photographed at the fuel pier on the south end of Dublon island. The vessel was not attacked here due to the high concentration of anti-aircraft guns in the vicinity.

As soon as it was discovered that the warships of the Combined Fleet had escaped the net, oil tankers were made the priority targets for US pilots. There is evidence to suggest that the tanker attacked by divebombers near the North Pass later on the same day, was the *Fujisan Maru*, trying to escape Truk Lagoon. It is widely accepted that the captain, having been attacked, was then made aware of the US attacking force nearby.

It seems he then ordered the ship about, and returned to a position in the Combined Fleet anchorage. During the second day of attacks, he then set a course for another escape attempt. The *Fujisan Maru* was very severely damaged by first one 1,000lb bomb, then another. Neither bomb hit, but they were close enough to the stern to cause the damage that can still be seen today. The ship was so rocked by these violent explosions that both deck guns were shorn from their mountings, and both anchors jolted from their housed position. The oil in her aft cargo holds caught fire, then the port anchor gained purchase on the bottom. With the engine on "full ahead", the vessel spun around before finally sinking. The putrid black smoke of her highly combustible cargo was then replaced by voluminous clouds of steam as the sea extinguished the fire.

The *Fujisan Maru* lay undetected for many decades until the Air Micronesian pilots Keith Jaeger and Ed O'Quinn noticed an oil slick south-east of Moen. Obtaining a fix on its location, the two later returned and found this wreck in 1976.

DIVING INFORMATION

THE forecastle supports a gun mount, but the deck gun has fallen off, either as a result of the nearby explosion, or during the sinking. The starboard anchor is incompletely stowed in the hawsepipe, while the port anchor chain is played out onto the seabed, and continues on underneath the hull of the wreck. The forecastle is connected to the midships superstructure by a catwalk above the cargo holds.

Moving aft of the forecastle, sizeable indentations will be seen in the starboard hull and port decking. Once thought to have been caused by pressure waves of bombs detonating in close proximity, it is more likely they have been caused by the buckling pressures of this depth. Just like an oversized drum, many crushed examples of which can be located on the wrecks in this lagoon, the forward holds of the *Fujisan Maru* were made to hold fuel, and therefore constructed to be equally air tight. There is photographic evidence that the bow of the *Fujisan Maru* was riding high in the water when it was by the fuel oil jetty at the south end of Dublon on the morning of February 17, 1944. This supports the theory that the forward oil tanks were nearly, or even completely, empty. As the vessel sank, some water may have got into her cargo tanks, but in the case of these holds forward of the bridge, the water did not get in fast enough to equalise the pressure, with the result that the cargo tanks – and consequently the hull of which they formed an integral part – were buckled by the increase of ambient pressure.

The midships superstructure and bridge is the shallowest part of the wreck at 37m. There was an anti-aircraft gun position on the top of this superstructure (indicated by finds of spent, and live rounds), but the weapon itself is no longer there. The beams are all that remains of the roof, otherwise the bridge is intact, with no visible damage. Inside the wheelhouse can be found a working ship's compass. The engine telegraph points clearly to the "full ahead" position. There are quantities of crockery underneath the bridge in a three-tier locker that rests with an assortment of other artefacts on a heap of sand and silt. Unfortunately some of the best pieces of decorated crockery have been stolen. Some however was rescued before it all disappeared, and is now waiting to be placed in the museum that is being established in Truk Lagoon. Other reported finds have been brass lanterns, a ship's clock, and a coffee grinder. The aft end of this superstucture is home to the ship's galley, which contains a triple stove and several artefacts in the silt on the port side.

Aft of the midships superstructure is a catwalk that connects this area with the stern castle. It runs over the aft cargo holds more or less on the starboard side of the ship.

The stern superstructure rises two decks above main deck. These decks are staggered. The interesting feature here is the devastation caused by the close proximity of a huge explosion. The smoke stack remains intact, but the decking and hull plating port of this funnel shows clearly why the ship sank. The stern gun, like its forward counterpart, is missing. The decking and structural elements here have collapsed due to either the explosion, or the very serious fire that burned as a result of that explosion. The intense heat of the fire is evidenced by metal railings that melted and drooped.

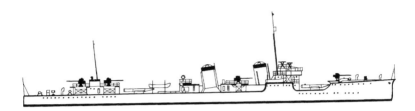

NAME:	FUMIZUKI.
TONNAGE:	1,913 (displacement, after conversion).
DIMENSIONS:	103.25m x 9.15m x 2.95m.
SHIP TYPE:	Mutsuki-class destroyer.
SUNKEN ATTITUDE:	Even keel. 15-20 degree list to port.
DEPTH TO SEABED:	38m.
DEPTH TO WRECK:	27m.
FEATURES OF NOTE:	4.7in gun on fo'csle. Torpedo launchers. Propellers.

BUILT by Fujinagata Zosen of Osaka, this Mutsuki class Destroyer No 29 was launched on February 16, 1926. According to the tradition of this class of warship, it received the name of the month in which it was commissioned, in this case Fumizuki, meaning July. The destroyer was actually completed and commissioned on July 3, 1926. This was the second *Fumizuki* in the Japanese Navy. The first, a Russian craft, was scuttled in 1904.

Attached to Destroyer Flotilla No. 5, the *Fumizuki* was based in Formosa (Taiwan). Her crew saw action during the Solomons campaign in the first few months of 1942, and the following year they and their vessel were part of the famous Tokyo Express, a convoy of ships sent from Japan to help in the relief of Guadalcanal. The *Fumizuki* was then posted to Rabaul.

The *Fumizuki* was damaged by attacking aircraft while en route to Kavieng on March 30, 1943, then a few days later was further damaged by another attack while she was escorting a convoy. The ship's plating was damaged amidships by a near miss, and one of her boiler rooms consequently flooded. Another air attack again damaged the *Fumizuki* on October 9, 1943, and three months later on January 4, 1944, while passing the Stephen Strait, she was attacked and damaged by planes from the US carriers *Bunker Hill* and *Monterey*. The warship's luck was running out, and several weeks after this attack, she was hit again, this time by B24 bombers carrying out a raid on the island of Rabaul. The destroyer now set sail for Truk and much-needed repairs.

Entering Truk lagoon in the evening of February 6, 1944, the *Fumizuki* anchored in the Combined Fleet anchorage north-west of Dublon island. The following day the destroyer was moved to a position near the fleet repair ship *Akashi*. According to Mr. Heigo Matsumoto the Chief Gunnery Officer, and Executive Officer of the *Fumizuki* during the attack, the vessel joined other ships such as the *Kensho Maru*, *Hoyo Maru*, *Kiyozumi Maru*, and *Tonan Maru No.3*, that like the *Fumizuki* had been damaged in attacks outside Truk – and like the *Fumizuki* were

Right: electrical switchgear in a container on the wreck of the Fumizuki.

all to be sunk during Operation Hailstone. When the American attack started on February 17, 1944, both engines of the *Fumizuki* had been stripped down for repairs, not all of the guns were serviceable, and most of the ship's ammunition had been removed. The destroyer survived the first wave, while engineers managed to re-assemble one of the ship's turbines. With only one of the propellers operational, the vessel then left its anchorage and was bombed at 10.30hrs the same day. None of the bombs made contact, but one 500lb device armed with a time-delay fuse detonated under water sufficiently close for the resulting pressure waves to deal the crippling blow. The ship's hull was sufficiently damaged on the port side of the aft engine room for flooding to start. The crew attempted damage control, but the ship listed then settled in the water. The only serviceable engine had been put out of action, so the starboard anchor was dropped to prevent the vessel from drifting onto the coral reefs nearby.

A request was then made for a tow to the naval station at Dublon, but this attempt failed, and finally the order was given to abandon ship. The crew was taken off by the tug that had come to the *Fumizuki*'s aid. The crew and officers were taken off in the early hours of February 18, and though the tug was then attacked, the crew of the *Fumizuki* managed to get to Dublon. They turned to watch their ship sink where she was anchored, at around 05.30 that same morning.

The wreck of the *Fumizuki* was located in April, 1987, by Japanese writer and diving enthusiast Tomoyuki Yoshimura. It lies west of Dublon, upright with a 20 degree list to port.

DIVING INFORMATION
IF photography is important to you, it is advisable to be among the first down on this site, as the *Fumizuki* has a fine dusting of grey silt all over it, which is virtually unnoticeable to anyone but a photographer.

The bow of the ship has very little rake, and the diver will notice that the only remaining anchor is the starboard one, and that this was deployed at the moment the vessel started to sink. The destroyer sank and finally came to rest with the anchor cable now crossing the bow of the ship. Two large capstans can be found, with the 4.7in dual-purpose bow gun on the focs'le. There is a collection of ammunition boxes all around this weapon, which still hold many live rounds ready for the breech. Being more substantially armoured than most other deck guns in the lagoon, and being less obscured by corals than the shallower wrecks, this weapon makes a good subject for photographs. On the port side of the gun's armour plating is a large tree of black coral. It is more than likely that the cabins in the focs'le below the gun are crews' quarters.

Located down on the well deck aft of the focs'le is an impressive triple torpedo launcher. As the ship was undergoing extensive repairs during the American attack it should come as no surprise that all tubes are empty of the 24in torpedoes it was designed to fire. It is possible to swim underneath the launcher and get a better look down the very large discharge tubes, as well as the huge gearing on which the launcher is traversed out to its firing position. The torpedoes were transported to this launcher on a narrow-gauge rail track which can be found on the starboard decking.

Due to a combination of corrosion, and the slight list of the wreck, along with the fact that an anchor from a large dive boat was dropped onto it in 1988, the bridge now hangs by a few sinews of metal upside down over the port side of the ship. The deck head of the bridge rests on the sea bed at 38m, and though it is a squeeze, it is possible to gain entry to this inverted part of the ship. This, however, is not recommended, due to the precarious nature of this part of the wreck, and the presence of silt. Looking in though, the destroyer's binnacle, gauges, voice tubes, and ship's compass are in a remarkable state of preservation.

Moving further aft, one of the smoke stacks remains in place and makes an impressive sight. Below it can be found an interesting collection of 13mm and larger anti-aircraft ammunition, both loose and in magazines. Sailors' uniforms, a ship's clock, a couple of navy model 93 gas masks, and a great deal of assorted crockery lying near a few large shells have been collected by divers over the years. The presence of several bombs in a rack nearby, with tail fins intact, makes a peculiar find on such a destroyer. There are reports that the engine room below this smoke stack contains human remains, but the entrance is very constricted.

Aft of the remaining smoke stack can be found the larger calibre anti-aircraft guns, and though their barrels have been removed, the armour plating remains, now supporting colourful corals. The deck and hull plating is quite visibly damaged at this part of the ship, either from bombs dropped on that fateful morning, or the ship hitting the seabed stern first.

Another 4.7in gun can be found on the stern of the *Fumizuki*. Below, the port propeller is all but totally buried in the silt and mud of the seabed. The starboard propeller, though, remains exposed, due to the list of the wreck, and makes an impressive sight.

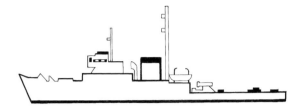

NAME:	FUTAGAMI.
TONNAGE:	625 (displacement).
DIMENSIONS:	40m x 9.6m x 3.1m.
SHIP TYPE:	Hashima Class salvage tug.
SUNKEN ATTITUDE:	Lies on a slope, with 45° list to port.
DEPTH TO SEABED:	18m-33m.
DEPTH TO WRECK:	15m to stern. 28m to bow.
FEATURES OF NOTE:	Bridge area and hold.

THIS large ocean-going tug was built in 1939 by Harima Sanbashi Co, of Aioi near Osaka, on the island of Honshu, Japan. Its 2,200ihp engine and twin propellers could drive the boat a maximum of 14.5 knots. Her complement of 59 could also protect themselves with two 25mm AA guns, and several depth charges. The *Futagami* was, however, primarily a salvage tug, and its crew more adept at operating the one 5-ton derrick, the two 2-ton derricks, or the salvage pumps. There is no information regarding the sinking of this and another tug during any attacks on Truk lagoon, and as there is documented evidence of two tugs surviving to the end of the war, it is possible the *Futagami* and the harbour tug were scuttled by either Japanese forces before the US arrival, or by US forces after seizure of the atoll.

DIVING INFORMATION

LYING between Dublon and Fefan, this wreck is very infrequently visited by divers. The visibility is not generally as good as it can be in the lagoon, but, as it is infrequently dived, any silt or sediment has not usually been previously disturbed by other diving groups.

Listing over to port and pointing down the very noticeable slope of the seabed, the first part usually seen is the rounded stern of the boat. This can be reached at a depth of just over 10m. The rudder points slightly starboard, and the twin three-bladed propellers are positioned on either side of the rudder post.

The aft hold requires careful finning techniques and a good torch. Finds include coils of hose. Two large racks hold 5m lengths of a wider 10cm diameter suction hose with brass couplings. These and the two large instruments, which are more than likely the salt-water pumps, would have been used to empty the ship's holds of any water they were taking in.

Moving forward, the large towing hook is located just aft of the engine room, and further forward still can be found the bridge. This is obviously smaller than the bridge areas of the larger wrecks, but none the less interesting because of that. One engine telegraph stands either side of the *Futagami*'s rudderstand. The vessel's compass surmounts the rudderstand, although the wheel itself is missing. Coral and sponge growth obscure many of the dials. Exhaled air along with stirred-up silt limit the time required to fully explore this navigation bridge, so it is recommended that this wreck is only visited by small groups of divers. The forward hold contains a large coil of rope in excellent condition, and it is in this part of the ship that the crews' quarters are located. Also of interest to divers is the deck pump mounted right on the bow. There is no visible damage to any of the wreck, which tends to support the theory that it was scuttled.

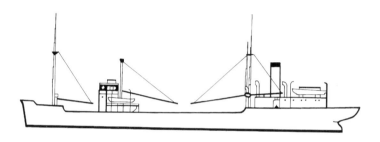

NAME:	GOSEI MARU.
TONNAGE:	1,931.
DIMENSIONS:	82.3m x 12.2m x 6.2m.
SHIP TYPE:	Freighter.
SUNKEN ATTITUDE:	Lies on port side on steep slope.
DEPTH TO SEABED:	36m (bow).
DEPTH TO WRECK:	2.5m (stern).
FEATURES OF NOTE:	Cargo of torpedoes, and torpedo damage.

BUILT by Tsurumi Seitetsu Zosen K.K. of Yokohama in 1937, this coastal freighter was owned by Koun Kisen K.K., but managed by the Yamashita Shipping Company. Its coal fired reciprocating steam engine was capable of driving the vessel a maximum of nearly 13 but more usually 10 knots.

The *Gosei Maru* was used for transporting torpedoes, and was doing just this for either the torpedo boat station on Uman and/or the 7th Flotilla of the 6th Submarine Fleet that had its headquarters in Truk. Attacked by bombers on the first day of Operation Hailstone, she was actually sunk by a torpedo hit from planes of the carrier *Monterey* during the second wave of February 18, 1944. The *Gosei Maru* was described by the American pilots as being "rusty and unkempt looking". The crew of the Avenger aircraft that launched the final torpedo saw the explosion, a fire, then the ship listed and sank. Residents of Uman reported several explosions on the wreck during 1976 and 1977 and these turned out to be due to the 8,000psi oxygen/air tanks of the torpedo cargo, rupturing because of corrosion. Due to the unpredictability of these explosions, and obvious danger to divers, charges were set and detonated on all remaining high-pressure tanks in April 1977. The wreck lies north-east of Uman island, pointing down a steep-sloping seabed, with a heavy list to port.

DIVING INFORMATION

DUE to the aspect of the wreck, it makes common sense to start the dive at the bow down at 36m, and work steadily up towards the shallower stern in only 2.5m. The description therefore starts at the bow. The bow is slightly raked, and the port anchor chain leads out to the seabed. The forecastle holds a windlass, and moving aft the foremast can be seen to be now broken off.

Number 1 hold is basically empty, but shows a great deal of damage from the torpedo that hit the ship here on the starboard side. The resulting explosion also damaged the forward superstructure. The plates and beams are all severely buckled and ripped around the hole caused by the torpedo.

The bridge is located on this forward superstructure, that stands two decks above the main deck. The cabins and bridge here have suffered not only from the explosion of the torpedo, but the ravages of time.

Number 2 hold is preceded by the remains of a large kingpost and two deck winches used for handling cargo (50 gallon drums and torpedoes, which shifted forward and across to the port side of the hold during the sinking). These 21in torpedos are without their warheads, which are stowed in the lower parts of the holds. The high-pressure tanks of these torpedoes contained either oxygen or compressed air, depending on the model.

The aft superstructure contains many cabins that are easily explored, containing the usual beer and sake bottles, as well as various items of crockery. Due to the appreciably shallower depth here, there is far more ambient light than on the deeper portions of the ship. The engine room is relatively easy to get to. With the wreck on its port side, orientation can be a bit of a problem for some divers, so this should be borne in mind before any exploration. The wooden decking of the upper boatsdeck was either burned away before sinking, or has rotted with time, but the deck and bulkhead beams remain intact, supporting much coral growth. The metal of the straight smoke stack is rotting and collapsing in places. The lifeboat davits remain in place, but a more interesting and very photogenic subject is the four-bladed coral-covered propeller and rudder under the beautiful lines of the ship's clipper stern.

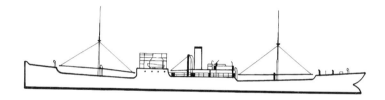

NAME: HANAKAWA MARU.
TONNAGE: 4,793.
DIMENSIONS: 112m x 15.8m x 9.1m.
SHIP TYPE: Passenger-Cargo.
SUNKEN ATTITUDE: Even keel on sloping bottom.
DEPTH TO SEABED: 34m.
DEPTH TO WRECK: 15m (the bridge).
FEATURES OF NOTE: Coral growth. The still leaking
aviation fuel or other caustic substance may
result in burns to unprotected skin.

BUILT by the Kawasaki Dockyard of Kobe, the *Hanakawa Maru* was launched on August 31, 1943. The ship was owned by Kawasaki Kisen Kaisha, its 2,000hp engine capable of driving it up to 15 knots.

The *Hanakawa Maru* was reportedly offloading troops onto the island of Tol when it was attacked by planes on the second day of attacks at Truk Lagoon. With a cargo of fuel drums, it is no surprise that following the first torpedo hit by planes from the carriers *Bunker Hill* and *Monterey*, there was an explosion, then a fierce fire as fuel drums ruptured, their high octane contents feeding the inferno that engulfed the vessel. The *Hanakawa* sank in three minutes, leaving a pool of burning fuel that drifted onto the nearby island of Tol.

DIVING INFORMATION

BEFORE any dive on this wreck, all divers must be aware of the presence of a caustic substance still leaking out from an unknown location on the ship. This substance can cause temporary but uncomfortable burns to unprotected skin. Secondly, it takes over 75 minutes to travel to the wreck site from Moen.

Still under tension, the anchor chain can be seen running out of its hawse pipe in the bow. There is no deck gun on the bow, which, along with the forecastle, is covered in splendid corals. These include an unusually high number of black corals. The coral growth on the entire deck and sides of this wreck is wonderful.

Number 1 hold contains a few drums on the upper levels. The hatch covers and beams are missing, allowing easy access into the hold itself (although this is not recommended). Like the drums on the *Hoki Maru*, the ones here could contain aviation fuel. Whatever they contain, it is reasonable to assume that an approach from above would place the diver in the path of any substance floating to the surface.

Any investigation of them would therefore require an approach at an oblique angle. Cargo winches and some ventilator shafts are all that remain on the main deck between holds 1 and 2. Following the torpedo hit on the starboard side of hold 2, there was an explosion that blew at least one cargo derrick, some hatch covers and several of the cargo of drums out of the vessel. These now lie on the seabed on the port side of the wreck. Number 2 hold contains more drums similar to those found in the first hold, and therefore requires the same amount of care when entering. The hole blasted by the torpedo on the starboard side is an impressive sight, and gives an idea of the awesome power used to sink this ship. The hull plates ruptured and torn here all point inwards from the force of the explosion, and this feature can easily be viewed from outside the ship, reducing the risk of burns.

The midship superstructure consists of three levels. Access from the bow area is by two doorways, one on either side. The lower level appears to have been some sort of rest area for the crew, and given its proximity to the torpedo hit, it should come as no surprise that this area contains human remains. The second deck level of this superstructure is recessed to allow a passageway down both starboard and port sides. The communications room is located here, with racks of radio equipment and wiring sharing deck space with a huge gorgonia fan coral. The deck above this returns to the full width of the ship again. Here you will find the navigation bridge. Above this, at a depth of 16m, would have been the flying bridge. Little now remains of this. The wooden decking of the bridge was probably destroyed during the fire on board. The rudder stand remains, although it is obscured by soft corals. Number 3 hold is raised one deck above the other holds of the ship, and separates the midship superstructure. This hold is appreciably smaller than the other four holds of the vessel. An open doorway in this hold allows access to the engine room, which is located under the next part of the superstructure.

The aft end of the midship superstructure rises only one deck above main deck level. Little remains now of the smoke stack. The skylight house, located aft of the funnel, has two skylights each side, leading down to the engine room. Lifeboat davits remain pointing inboard, demonstrating the speed with which this ship went down. It is in this part of the ship that the toilets, cabins, and ship's galley are located. This latter is situated on the port side, one deck below main deck level. It contains a stove, more examples of crockery, bottles, and a large bowl used for cooking rice. Human remains are also located in this part of the ship, so divers are asked to be respectful of any bones they see. Access to the engine room is made easy by open doors and there are catwalks and gantries facilitating penetration to lower levels. The silt, however, is very bad in this part of the wreck.

Hold numbers 4 and 5 contain more of the cargo of drums seen in the forward holds. Lying across the top of the hatch, the cargo derricks of both holds point to port. Several drums have floated, or been blown out onto the deck.

The coral-covered sterncastle is worth a visit to see the extraordinary 4.7in anti-submarine gun mounted on a circular gun platform. Pointing upwards, it is surrounded by colourful corals. Also in the quarters here have been found more drums or depth charges, and artillery shells.

Opposite: crockery and
beer bottles, Nippo Maru.

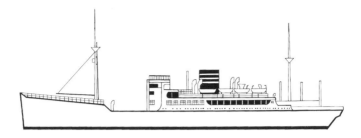

NAME:	HEIAN MARU.
TONNAGE:	11,616.
DIMENSIONS:	155.44m x 20.11m x 9.14m.
SHIP TYPE:	Submarine tender.
SUNKEN ATTITUDE:	Lies on port side.
DEPTH TO SEABED:	35m.
DEPTH TO WRECK:	13m (starboard beam).
FEATURES OF NOTE:	Submarine periscopes along starboard passageway. Ship's name on bow, in both English and Kanji writing.

COSTING $15million, the *Heian Maru* was built by Nippon Yusen Kaisha (NYK) of Osaka, in 1930. Incorporating the latest "Old English" style interior, the *Heian Maru*, along with her two sister ships the *Hikawa Maru*, and the *Hiye Maru*, was built as a passenger cargo ship for the trans-Pacific run to Seattle. Launched on April 16, 1930, her maiden voyage from Hong Kong to Seattle did not take place until January the following year. The ship's two 8-cylinder Burmeister & Wain diesel engines generated 13,404 horsepower, driving the vessel at a maximum of 18.38 knots. It was this power that set a new trans-Pacific record for the NYK line. On arriving at Seattle, the owners of the ship let members of the public tour her. So popular was the *Heian Maru*, that almost 15,000 people are reputed to have viewed her, with hundreds more being turned away. Just over 14 years later she would be sunk by Americans.

Recalled from Seattle in August 1941, three months before Pearl Harbour, the *Heian Maru* underwent a conversion into a submarine tender. In October of that year the ship was commissioned into the Sixth Submarine Fleet as a tender, based at Kwajalein.

By February 17, 1944 the Sixth Submarine Fleet had taken a great number of losses. Two days later, it had lost two more vessels, for the *Heian Maru* and the submarine *Shinohara* lay at the bottom of the seabed as a result of Operation Hailstone.

At anchor just off the northwest shore of Dublon, Japanese sources report the *Heian Maru* being hit by a bomb near Number 6 hold, at 06.55 on the February 17, which coincides with the US reports of aircraft from the carrier *Yorktown* bombing three ships west of Dublon at around 06.30. Later strafed by Hellcats about 10.10, the *Heian Maru* was gradually consumed by fire. With flames threatening to reach and detonate the cargo of torpedoes in the forward hold, and unable to extinguish the blaze, most of the crew was given the order to abandon ship in the early hours of February 18. After several near misses, the ship then received two bomb hits aft, and later in the day was struck by one, maybe two torpedoes from aircraft of the carrier *Bunker Hill*. With the vessel already beginning to list, the one or two torpedoes that slammed into the ship's port side near the engine room were all that was needed to finally sink the *Heian Maru*. There are no reports of any US pilots seeing the ship sink, but an intercepted Japanese radio message gave the time of her sinking as 15.03. The *Heian Maru* went down with the loss of two people, and 28 wounded.

DIVING INFORMATION
LYING on its port side in 35m of water, the *Heian Maru* is intact, but with less coral growth than most other wrecks. As always in wrecks in this attitude, orientation is a problem, and deep penetration of the wreck is not recommended.

The starboard side of the bow at 21m provides a convenient resting place to sort out gauges and check bouyancy, and the lack of coral leaves the ship's name, in both Kanji and English letters, exposed. While the starboard anchor is housed, the port anchor chain leads out of the hawsepipe and stretches out along the seabed, coming to an end at a large mooring buoy to which the chain is attached. This large, cylindrical, mooring buoy was dragged down with the vessel during the sinking. Alongside this, can be found one of the three older anchors used to hold the buoy in place. Also nearby can be seen two lengths of chain and an electrical cable running towards Dublon. Moving aft along the starboard beam, impressive lines of portholes come into view, and these, along with the ship's name, are very photogenic. Continuing on and up into shallower water, along the starboard plating of the hull, there is little marine life other than swarms of onionskin algae. Finning over the rails to the main deck, which lies at right angles to the seabed, there is a platform for a bow gun, but no such artillery piece is in evidence. Spent shell casings can be found, and suggest that there was a gun here at some time. Two windlasses are located underneath this large gun platform.

Numbers 1 and 2 holds are difficult to get into as most of the hatch covers are in place. They contain more ammunition and cannisters. The winch house between these holds is as wide as the ship, with passageways down both port and starboard sides. The forward mast and ventilators protrude from the top of this structure, with the coral-covered mast extending out over the seabed. Several torpedo warheads are located in this area.

The midship superstructure has a slightly curved frontage, and is three decks high. It used to be four decks high, but the wooden flying bridge is no longer there. Most of the contents of these decks has fallen to the port side, and now lies on the bottom at 35m. Finds include binoculars, boxes and unopened chests, crockery, bottles, and an AA gun. Inside the bridge, looking up towards the surface you can see an impressive, long line of square windows arcing up towards the surface. As the ship did not sink until a day and a half after the fire had started, there is extensive heat damage on decking, portholes, and even metal. One fascinating cargo of this ship relatively undamaged by the blaze, though, is located along the passageways of this superstructure. It is a consignment of replacement periscopes for the Sixth Submarine Fleet. With the lower part of these periscopes still carrying the fold-away handles and eye-pieces, this end of all the periscopes looks remarkably chunky in comparison to the upper portion that tapers to a slender tip, in which only a small mirror is located. It is easy to imagine a Japanese submarine commander, arms draped over the periscope handles, as he watched some unfortunate allied ship sink before him. The fact that these periscopes were in turn torpedoed and sunk along with the torpedoes stored aft, lends a poetic justice to it all. The periscopes on the starboard gangways are at a depth of 19m.

Although plenty of ambient light makes finning through the superstructure relatively easy, divers must be cautioned about going as deep as the engine room. Here, not only orientation, but a tangle of hull plating, piping, beams, grating, damaged catwalks and the like from at least one torpedo explosion, pose a very real threat to unrestricted swimming. Little to no light at all penetrates as deep into the ship as this. A torch is absolutely vital for any exploration of this area.

The upper decks of the superstructure bulge upwards from the blasts of the torpedo explosions, and the smoke stack plating is also dented inwards, more than likely by the pressure waves of near misses. Lifeboat davits hang empty from the evacuation on the February 18, 1944, and a collection of air vents, fan housings, and engine-room skylights cram the boat deck. Abaft the funnel, the starboard hull, rippled by the near misses and torpedo hits, is the shallowest portion of the ship at 12m. A gangplank, roomy passageways, and portholes make this part of the wreck easy to explore.

Moving further aft, there is a king post, and a cargo hold, but access into this hold is prevented by the hatch covers, which remain in place. On the seabed here can be found a huge old anchor, and the barrel of a deck gun, both partially buried in the sand.

Further aft still, the deck level is lowered yet again, with another gun lying next to a mooring cleat. Several more torpedoes can be found in the holds here, although their high-pressure tanks have finally blown through the rotting metal carcass of the torpedo bodies. Like its forward counterpart, the winch house here covers the full width of the vessel, with passageways through its port and starboard sides. Protruding from the top of this, the aft mast and cross tree lean out parallel to the seabed.

The poop deck supports a huge gun platform, but the artillery piece itself is missing. Moving over the starboard deck rails of the ship, and following the hull down to a depth of 26m, there are two very impressive propellers, and a large rudder.

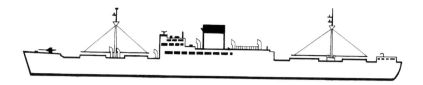

NAME:	HINO MARU No 2 (Gun high wreck).
TONNAGE:	999.
DIMENSIONS:	61m x 5.2m x 4.8m.
SHIP TYPE:	Armed freighter.
SUNKEN ATTITUDE:	Upright (10 degree list to starboard).
DEPTH TO SEABED:	9m (bow) 21m (stern).
DEPTH TO WRECK:	1m (to the bow gun).
FEATURES OF NOTE:	Bow gun.

BUILT by Mitsubishi Heavy Industries and launched on September 16, 1935, the *Hino Maru No 2* was a small freighter, with a single diesel engine capable of driving it up to 12.5 knots. Believed to have been sunk during the carrier-based raids of April 29-30, 1944, a wreck about 125m west of Uman is probably that of the *Hino Maru No 2*, although to date, there has been no positive identification to this effect.

DIVING INFORMATION

USUALLY used as a snorkelling site by the diving companies in Truk, this site is typically visited around midday, some time after the first dive. With the sun high in the sky, this makes photography very easy. The bow gun, devoid of much coral growth, is clearly visible from the surface, and has become the quintessential symbol of Truk Lagoon diving, appearing on T-shirts, letter headings, advertisements, and in many books.

The forward hold remains recognisable, along with the forward mast, which has collapsed over to starboard, but much of the decking and hull of this ship is very rusty. Not far from the top of this mast are the wrecks of some sort of railway carriage, and a small engine-powered wooden boat.

The superstructure was evidently destroyed by a large explosion, which has consequently exposed most of the engine room, and the diesel engine. The wreck therefore gives the distinct impression of being in two parts.

Lying in the deeper water of this submarine slope, the aft area of the wreck, too, is heavily damaged, although exploration of the interconnecting hold Numbers 3 and 4 will yield some of the ordnance this vessel was carrying as cargo. The aft mast, like its forward counterpart, has fallen over. At a depth of 21m, the ship's propeller remains intact, although the rudder has broken loose and lies on the seabed nearby.

Overleaf: the Hino Maru's
bow gun, symbol of Truk diving.

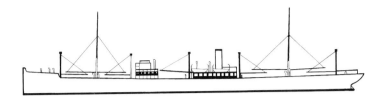

NAME:	HOKI MARU.
TONNAGE:	7,112.
DIMENSIONS:	137.25m x 17.75m x 9.57m.
SHIP TYPE:	Freighter.
SUNKEN ATTITUDE:	Even keel.
DEPTH TO SEABED:	56m.
DEPTH TO WRECK:	24m (midships).
FEATURES OF NOTE:	Bulldozers, trucks, and other equipment

in aft holds. (Risk of burns from some sort of caustic
substance around the wreck.)

BUILT in 1921 by William Denny & Brothers, of Dumbarton, Scotland, this five-hold freighter was powered by two engines made by the North British Diesel Company of Glasgow. The twin screws were capable of generating some 3,550 hp. Launched on November 28, the MV *Hauraki* was originally named after an inlet in North Island, New Zealand, and was built for the Union Steamship Corporation of that country.

At about 21.50 on July 12, 1942, whilst sailing between Freemantle, Australia, and Colombo in Ceylon, the MV *Hauraki* was boarded and captured by men from the *Aikoku* and the *Hokoku Maru*s. Using searchlights to illuminate both the stern gun and the bridge, Japanese marines armed with swords, automatic weapons and grenades, seized control of this passenger-freighter. Despite members of the crew throwing vital tools overboard, pumping over one hundred tons of fuel into the sea, and the chief engineer ordering his men to cease all maintenance work, the MV *Hauraki* was put into Singapore, and its crew interned.

The Japanese carried out several alterations, and re-named the vessel the *Hoki Maru* on December 31, 1942. The ship sailed from Yokohama in January, 1944, and arrived in Truk Lagoon later that month. The subject of several attacks throughout the morning of February 17, 1944, it was in the early afternoon that the *Hoki Maru* received a torpedo hit on the port beam. The resulting increase in an already established fire on board ignited drums of aviation fuel, which consequently exploded. The forward part of the ship became an inferno of burning fuel, and this released a thick cloud of black smoke. By dawn the next day, the vessel had sunk east of Eten island.

DIVING INFORMATION

DISCOVERED in 1973, the wreck site of the *Hoki Maru* was subsequently lost, then rediscovered in 1980. Today the wreck is visited by few divers, because of the risk of burning caused by some sort of caustic substance. Believed to be aviation fuel leaking from the multitude of drums still in the ship's holds, this substance is invisible. It gathers underneath the decking of the wreck, and is disturbed by a diver's exhalation bubbles. For this reason, the risk of burns increases proportionally to the number of divers on the wreck.

Although in a depth of 50m, the mast of this ship is visible beneath the surface of the water. Much of the wreck can be dived between 30-40m, because the main deck is around 30m.

The bow area carries two big windlasses. The starboard anchor is housed, and the port anchor is out. In his book *Hailstorm over Truk Lagoon*, Klaus Lindemann concludes that from the heap of anchor chain on the seabed below, the *Hoki Maru* sank rapidly. The very extensive damage in Number 2 hold bares this fact out.

Number 1 hold is not as damaged as Number 2, but the whole forward section of the *Hoki Maru* is a tangled area of utter devastation. This centres around the area of a huge explosion in Number 2 hold, produced either by a combination of torpedo and fuel cargo, or by a much later secondary detonation of the fuel cargo during a fire. There is no decking left in this part of the ship. All king posts, cargo derricks, and masts are either missing or part of the wreckage.

The superstructure was only one deck above main deck level, and the forward section, including the bridge, is twisted up and to starboard from the explosion in hold Number 2. The smoke stack has been blown from its original position, and now lies on the starboard side. The engine room skylights have also been blown open from a blast within. Much of the decking has collapsed midships, making any serious exploration very dangerous. The midship's hold, Number 3, is also severely damaged, with much wreckage from the blast.

Number 4 hold contains a plethora of beer bottles, some spare aeroplane propellers, engine blocks, and large fuel-oil drums, some of which have retained their air-tight integrity, only to be crushed by the greater water pressure at this depth of 40m. At main deck level, between the two aft holds, on the port side, is a heap of railway track.

Number 5 hold alone is worth the dive on this wreck, for it resembles a multi-level lorry park. By any standards, the now historic collection of vehicles in this hold is impressive. Diving down between the hatch-cover beams below the main deck to the first 'tween deck of this hold, there is a caterpillar tractor unit or prime mover. As your eyes get accustomed to the reduced light levels in here, it is possible to make out another caterpillar tractor unit, two lorries relatively intact, and two bulldozers. These last two are a real surprise, for the Japanese did not tend to use such equipment. They prefered to use slave labour for earth moving. Certainly US intelligence at the time knew of no Japanese manufactured bulldozer. It is a reasonable assumption, therefore, that these units were captured from the allies. Various engines and compressors can also be found here.

Descending to the second 'tween deck at a depth of 38m, there are six more lorries, a four-wheeled agricultural style tractor, and a steam roller. There is also what appears to be bomb or torpedo damage in the starboard side of the hull here. Two types of lorry can be found here, and one is definitely the 1941, Toyoda Model 1 4x2, 6-cylinder truck, which weighed 5,500lb (and was an almost exact copy of the 1939 US Chevrolet truck). The second, more angular type, may well be the 1934, Model 94, 6x4, 6-cylinder truck. The fact that most of the headlamps are smoke blackened on the inside, several lumps of molten glass can be found inside the cabs, and there is evidence of charring on the wooden interior, points to this deck being involved in some sort of fire before sinking. Despite this, these lorries, particularly the Toyodas with their graceful curves, bullnosed radiators, intact tyres, and huge headlamps, are very photogenic.

These vehicles are all stowed tightly into this 'tween deck, and it is necessary at times to swim between vehicle and deck head. This reduction in space also necessitates the use of wide-angle lenses when using a camera. Because the wreck is infrequently visited, there are plenty of rusticles stalactiting their way down from the iron deck levels above. These disintegrate in exhaled air bubbles, raining down as a rusty dust, which joins the silt rising from the deck beneath. It is therefore more essential than usual for any photographers to get there first.

The third 'tween deck below this contains some of the *Hoki Maru*'s cargo of aviation fuel in large metal drums.

The stern is of the clipper style, and therefore considerably overhangs the ship's two propellers and rudder. A flagpole remains in its position on the stern, though bent from the blast of a near-miss on February 17, 1944. More damage from this bomb is visible around the starboard side of the stern area.

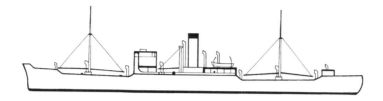

NAME:	HOKUYO MARU.
TONNAGE:	4,217.
DIMENSIONS:	108m x 15m x 9m.
SHIP TYPE:	Freighter.
SUNKEN ATTITUDE:	Upright.
DEPTH TO SEABED:	58-60m.
DEPTH TO WRECK:	50m (to deck).
FEATURES OF NOTE:	Bridge area.

BUILT in 1936 by the Uraga Dock Company Ltd of Tokyo Bay, the *Hokuyo Maru* is a freighter with five holds. The coal-fired turbine engine, and single screw, were capable of driving the ship up to 16 knots. It appears the ship was attacked on both days of Operation Hailstone, finally sinking after two 1,000lb bomb hits, on February 18, 1944.

DIVING INFORMATION

THE bow area is in good condition, with the port anchor out, and the starboard anchor retracted. The deck railing, winch mechanisms, windlass, and two mooring cleats are relatively void of all marine growth, because of the very great depth here. There is a spare anchor to be found on the forecastle bulkhead.

Number 1 hold contains solidified bags of cement under its hatch cover beams, but because the depth here is 51m, little exploration has been undertaken below main deck level.

The foremast and crosstree are located between Number 1 hold and Number 2 hold. Two ventilator cowls, and the booms, or cargo derricks, are largely intact, and the winch house that operated these, has two doorways facing aft. Number 2 hold appears to contain little of interest. The midship's superstructure is interesting to dive around, because the bridge on the third deck still contains many of the original instruments. These include two telegraphs, a rudder stand and wheel, and the ship's compass. There are reports of a torpedo hole in the starboard side of the hull here, although the depth is currently beyond the limit of sports divers.

Number 3 hold is appreciably smaller than the others on board, and the decking around this area of the ship has been burned away following the fires started on February 17, 1944. At the aft end of this hold can be found the small rectangular coal chute. The markings on the smoke stack, which still stands, are those of the

Kita Nikon Kisen line, who owned the vessel before it was requisitioned by the Japanese Navy. The empty lifeboat davits, and exposed deck support beams, seem to add to the general air of chaos here. Aft of midships there is plenty of buckled metalwork and fire damage. The starboard hull plates were ruptured outwards here when the boiler exploded, so it is highly unlikely that much remains of the engine room.

The stern area of the vessel shows a great deal of damage from at least one, but maybe two large explosions that seem to originate from the port side around Number 5 hold. Bulkheads, plating and decking here are bent and twisted from these explosions.

NAME:	HOYO MARU.
TONNAGE:	8,691.
DIMENSIONS:	144.7m x 18.5m x 9.1m.
SHIP TYPE:	Oil tanker.
SUNKEN ATTITUDE:	Capsized on sloping seabed.
DEPTH TO SEABED:	34m at stern.
DEPTH TO WRECK:	3m (to hull).
FEATURES OF NOTE:	Propeller and rudder. Coral growths.

THE *Hoyo Maru* was built in 1936 by Mitsubishi Jukogyo, of Yokohama. This tanker has a single screw, and powered by its 1,163nhp diesel engine, was capable of speeds up to a maximum of 16 knots. The ship was commandeered by the Japanese Navy in 1940, and having been armed with two 80mm deck guns for the bow and stern, was stationed in Truk a year later.

The tanker took part in the invasion of New Guinea during April and May of 1942, and survived the Battle of the Coral Sea. Japanese reports claim that on March 31, 1942, while 20 miles north-west of Rabaul, the *Hoyo Maru* sank a US submarine, but the US has no record of such a loss. The *Hoyo Maru* received bomb damage in 1943, and was hit by a torpedo in late 1943. The bomb damage was repaired in Japan by Hitachi Zosen, and completed in July 1943. Then, while sailing from Singapore with supplies, the *Hoyo Maru* was torpedoed. The US submarine scored one hit in the early hours of November 6, 1943. This disabled the engines. The *Hoyo Maru* was towed into Truk, where her fuel cargo was unloaded. The vessel was then towed to the repair anchorage north-west of Fefan island, where it spent over four months undergoing repairs before being bombed and capsized, on February 17, 1944. The *Hoyo Maru* did not sink for several months after, remaining "keel up", in the same position, 400m north-east of Fefan.

DIVING INFORMATION

ALTHOUGH capsized, this is an interesting wreck, because it is absolutely smothered in colourful marine life, and lies only 3m below the surface. This depth increases down to a seabed of 34m at the stern.

The bow area has a buckled gun platform, but no sign of the 80mm deck gun. The ship's name in English and Japanese characters is partly visible. The anchor is paid out, which probably means the ship did not, or could not, move during the attacks. Because there is a 4m gap between the upside-down decking and the seabed, access into the foc'sle cabins is good. With the ship being upside down, orientation is difficult, and there is very little ambient light, so a torch is crucial for any serious exploration here. There are two fine examples of ships' lanterns, as well as coils of steel cable, plenty of fish, and even some lobsters.

There are two fine examples of ships' lanterns on the Hoyo Maru.

Behind the forecastle, the deck of the *Hoyo Maru* has many pipes and valve fittings for the loading and discharging of the fuel cargo. There is also a raised catwalk or gantry, running along the length of all the cargo holds.

Moving further aft, at a much shallower depth of only 3m, there is a sizeable split right across the ship's hull. The coral growths here, particularly around the bilge keels on either side of the ship, are excellent, branches of red soft coral and stretches of jeweller's coral being especially photogenic.

Access into the midships superstructure can be made from either the port or starboard. Both sides of the *Hoyo Maru* are clear of the seabed here. Again, orientation inside the passages and cabins is difficult because of everything being upside down, and there is a lot of silt on all the deckheads or cabin ceilings.

Continuing aft, under about 50m of cargo holds, piping, valves and catwalk, and over the bomb-damaged decks, the aft superstructure will be reached. The mess of twisted plating, buckled bulkheads, and general scene of destruction inside this is due to further bomb hits here. This superstructure is larger than that at midships, and it is here that the engine room is located. A contributing factor towards all this damage can be seen if the diver ascends up to a position on the port side of the ship's hull. At a depth of 15m, fairly near the stern, there is a very large hole in the shell plating. With all the jagged edges of this pointing inwards, it is a fairly reasonable assumption that this is where the torpedo struck on November 6, 1943. Swimming inside this, the diver will see the tangled mess of the engine room, a junkyard of pipes, gauges, catwalks, and heavy machinery. The engine has fallen from its mountings to the skylights below, and cylinders, fuses, drums, switch gear, and even a couple of shoes can be found here.

Right at the stern, at a depth of 20m, is the impressive, and very large, four-bladed propeller, along with the coral-covered rudder.

Lying in a north-east-south-west direction, this tanker is almost 150m long. This length, combined with the maximum seabed depth of 34m, makes any serious attempt to cover the entire shipwreck on a single dive very difficult. It therefore makes sense to plan the end of any dive midships along the hull, which is at a convenient depth of only 3m. The abundance of coral growth here makes decompression stops a pleasure.

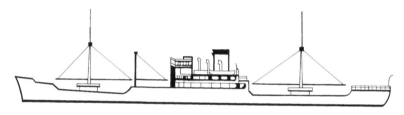

NAME:	KENSHO MARU.
TONNAGE:	4,861.
DIMENSIONS:	384.4m x 52.5ft/30.3m.
SHIP TYPE:	Passenger cargo.
SUNKEN ATTITUDE:	20 degree list to port.
DEPTH TO SEABED:	40m (stern).
DEPTH TO WRECK:	7.5m (masthead).
FEATURES OF NOTE:	Bow gun. Interesting bridge area.

BUILT in 1938, by Tama Sanbashi Co, this five-hold freighter had a single screw powered by one 642nhp diesel engine. Originally owned by Inui Kisen K.K. of Kobe near Osaka, the *Kensho* or *Kansho Maru* was commandeered by the Japanese Navy on September 15, 1940, for war service. It is thought the bow gun and platform were probably installed some time in 1942. Shortly after this, modifications were made to parts of the smaller Number 3 hold, to convert it into a sick bay and X-ray room. Extra medical staff were then added to the gun crew and ship's complement. The *Kensho Maru* was then used to carry supplies to the Marshall Islands, and wounded personnel back to Japan.

The ship was bombed while offloading stores at Kwajalein, (in the Marshalls) some time in December, 1943. Two sailors in the engine room were killed, and the vessel was beached to prevent its sinking. Fires on board were extinguished, and some elementary repairs made. On January 3, 1944, the *Kensho Maru* was towed to Truk Lagoon for major repairs. She was seen by US pilots, with the repair ship *Akashi Maru*, at the repair anchorage.

Unable to move their crippled ship out of the danger of Operation Hailstone, the crew of the *Kensho Maru* took to the lifeboats, and rowed ashore to Dublon in the west. The unmanned ship was reported to have been hit amidships on the first morning of attacks. This 1,000lb bomb explosion subsequently started a fire that raged for many hours. The ship was still afloat the following day, but received a torpedo hit in the morning of February 18.

The wreck of the *Kensho Maru* was found by Klaus Lindemann, or rather his wife, almost by accident on June 24, 1980. Until it was formerly identified as the *Kensho Maru*, it had been known as the *Mary D Maru*, after the lady who first found it.

The ship lies north-east of Fefan, and west of Dublon.

DIVING INFORMATION

THE raked bow points north-west, and is in good condition. The starboard anchor was out at the time of sinking, and the anchor chain for this still leads out of the hawse pipe and down around the bow on the seabed. At a depth of 22m, the fore-castle carries a large gun platform surmounted by an impressive 3in deck gun. Three full and half full crates of shells lie around the breech mechanism, and the ordnance has a light covering of corals, and other marine growth. The wooden deck boards of this gun platform have since rotted away, but this feature of the ship is still worth a visit. Also on the forecastle are the winch and take-up drum for operating the ship's two anchors. Moving aft, and descending to Number 1 hold, the port and starboard doors into the forecastle are shut fast, and so far deny access into the forward cabins.

All of the three forward holds are empty of cargo, but many of their hatch beams remain in place. The foremast is covered in soft and hard corals, and is located between holds 1 and 2. There is also a large masthouse that was evidently used for storing many of the ship's ropes and cables. As well as these items, there is a spare anchor bolted to the masthouse bulkhead, on the starboard side. Because the vessel is tilting to port, many of the cargo derricks have also now swung to port. There is evidence too, of there having been at least one, maybe two explo-sions near the ship here, for the decking is buckled, deck support beams are bent, and the outside shell plating is rippled on both sides. Number 3 hold is elevated one deck above main deck, and aft of the kingpost and a set of cargo winches. This hold is empty of cargo.

The midships superstructure is one deck level higher again than Number 3 hold, except for the bridge area, which is two decks higher. Because of the arte-facts to be found here, this is definitely the most interesting area of the wreck. Starting from the top, at a depth of 19m, the diver immediately notices that there is very little left of the bridge roof. Inside the bridge, there is an engine telegraph at the "full stop" position, the ship's helm (although the wooden wheel has since rot-ted), and a binnacle with ship's compass. Mounted on a circular stand, there are also some very long, high-powered binoculars, with the rubber eyepieces still intact. At the back of the bridge was a typewriter with English keys instead of Japanese characters. There is also a large loop antenna that has fallen from the roof above. This was evidently used for the two very large radio stacks located on the deck beneath the bridge. One of these stacks has fallen over, and there is a tan-gle of wiring that would have been secured to the deckhead. The knobs, dials, and even the kanji characters on the metal instruction plates are clearly visible, as well as the large valves inside. This radio shack was also used as the captain's chart room, and reported finds include a set of dividers, a sextant, a brass and enamel morse key, a srongbox, a set of reindeer antlers, and a smaller pair of binoculars in a metal drawer.

Descending through the deck levels of the *Kensho Maru*, the light drops off quite markedly. The portholes are all intact, but due to the marine growth on the glass, and even on days of good visibility, any exploration of the ship's interior really requires a torch. This is an exciting wreck to swim around in, and its cabin areas rate as some of the best to explore in the lagoon. The forward compartments of the superstructure can be exited on the port side at the main deck level of 29m. Continuing exploration of the ship's interior will yield the ship's head, collections of assorted plates, sake dishes, rice bowls, beer bottles, and lanterns.

Aft of the bridge, the vessel's large funnel dominates the entire scene on the boat deck. There are remains of the ventilators on the boat deck, but none of their cowls remains in place. Previous divers have made this the area to examine their finds from below decks, and while each item is now divorced from its original position during the sinking, and therefore of less historical interest to the inquisitive diver, there is a high concentration of finds in a very small area. All these items are now lined up near the engine room skylights on the starboard side, and include another typewriter, assorted bottles, plates, jugs, dishes, a teapot, and several lanterns. Access into the nearby engine room is via the companionways from the passages inside the ship, or from the twin rows of five skylights aft of the funnel. Needless to say, light levels in the engine room are very low, and a torch is a prerequisite of any serious exploration. The various gantries and catwalks are in good condition, as is the one B&W diesel engine, with its array of six cylinder heads. A spare piston may be found here also. Examination of the various gauges, dials, and instruments will reveal the glass over each to be smoke-blackened and stained by a long burning, smouldering, ship-board fire. Had the burning been more intense, then the glass of all these gauges would have been shattered, or melted. The depth at the cylinder heads is 27m.

The empty davits stand as mute reminders of the crew's exit, and below these can be found the *Kensho Maru*'s galley. A big stove, quantities of assorted crockery, a fan, and boxes of bottles remain where they were left during an air raid on February 17, 1944.

Number 4 hold contains a large compressor on the port side 'tween deck, and a consignment of books, which though waterlogged, remain remarkably intact. The aft masthouse separates this hold with Number 5 hold, and is just as spacious as its forward counterpart. As with the forward cargo derricks, the ones here have also swung down with the 20 degree tilt to port. There is a small winch house between the two aft holds, and this is full of electric motors, cabling, and switch gear. The aft mast provides an interesting diversion all the way up to just 7.5m from the surface. Such shallow coral-laden features are ideal for ending the dive or whiling away any decompression stop.

Number 5 hold contains a heap of bicycles, lengths of pipework, and rows of several very ominous-looking gas cylinders. The inevitable corrosion of time will soon reduce the wall thickness of these cylinders to a dangerous point where the greater pressure within causes them to explode. Divers are therefore advised to treat this cargo with respect.

The stern castle shows bomb damage to the shell plating and decking, and access into the cabins of this part of the ship can be made either by the starboard door of the forward bulkhead, by the open skylights on the upper deck, or by the hole in the decking caused by a bomb hit. It is thought that this was the damage sustained in Kwajalein the month before Operation Hailstone. Certainly it would have seriously affected the gears, and steering mechanisms to be found in the cabins here. The stern itself is of the "clipper" variety, and leads down to a single four-bladed propeller.

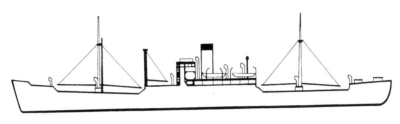

NAME:	KIKUKAWA MARU.
TONNAGE:	3,833.
DIMENSIONS:	108.1m x 15.2m x 8.3m.
SHIP TYPE:	Passenger cargo.
SUNKEN ATTITUDE:	Lies on starboard side.
DEPTH TO SEABED:	36m.
DEPTH TO WRECK:	20m (port beam).
FEATURES OF NOTE:	Aircraft parts. Compressor. Truck remains.

BUILT in 1937 by Kawasaki Dockyards in Kobe, this five-hold freighter had a single propeller driven by two engines. These generated 333nhp. The ship was capable of a maximum speed of nearly 15 knots, and a service speed of about 12. Before being taken over for military use, the vessel was owned by the Kawasaki Kisen line.

During 1943, while loaded with cargo from Japan, the *Kikukawa Maru* put into Truk Lagoon. A serious fire broke out on board, and despite vigorous attempts from over 50 personnel using many pumps on board, and dozens of little boats tied up alongside, the fire reached the cargo of ordnance. At around 18.30 on October 7, 1943, the ship exploded so violently that it killed all of the people on board and in the 40-50 boats tied alongside. The devastation was all but complete, for all that now remains are the bow, and the forward three holds.

The wreckage was found on June 16, 1976.

DIVING INFORMATION

THE shipwreck lies on its starboard beam, but all of the ship aft of Number 3 hold was destroyed in the explosion of 1943. The bow is raked, and both anchors are out, their chains buried in the silty bottom. The name of the vessel is welded onto the bow in both English and Japanese characters, but is now covered by algae.

Number 1 hold contains many bottles, and a couple of items of heavy machinery, compressor, and a pump, both on wheels. The latter was probably part of the fire fighting operations before the sinking. These items, along with the more numerous cargo of fuel oil drums in holds 1 and 2, have, of course, fallen over to starboard, and in some cases, out onto the seabed.

Number 3 hold contains an interesting array of spare parts for aeroplanes. These include fuselage parts, spare aero propellers, nose cone assemblies, under-carriage parts, and even radial engines. There is also the wreckage of a lorry here. Due to the sunken attitude of the *Kikukawa Maru*, much of this has tumbled on top of itself, giving it all the appearance of a scrap yard.

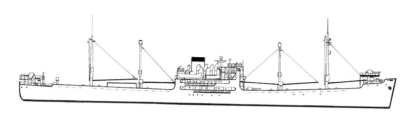

NAME:	KIYOSUMI MARU.
TONNAGE:	8,614.
DIMENSIONS:	138.2m x 18.5m x 8.5m.
SHIP TYPE:	Transport.
SUNKEN ATTITUDE:	Lies on port side.
DEPTH TO SEABED:	33.5m at stern.
DEPTH TO WRECK:	12m (starboard beam).
FEATURES OF NOTE:	Torpedo launchers aft. Bicycles.

BUILT in 1934, the *Kiyosumi Maru* entered service on October 5, 1934. This large, six-hold freighter has a single screw, which had been driven by a massive Mitsubishi-Sulzer diesel engine generating 8,375 hp. This meant it could attain a maximum speed of nearly 19 knots, and give a cruising speed of 15 knots. The ship was built by the Kawasaki Jyuko Co, near Tokyo, for the Kakusai Kisen line. It had a crew of 50, and cabin space for 12 passengers.

Commandeered by the Japanese military, the *Kiyosumi Maru* was fitted with eight 6in deck guns, several anti-aircraft machine guns, and torpedo launchers. Thus converted into an armed merchant cruiser in August 1941, the ship was used as a troop transporter. It went on to see action in the battle of Midway Island during May-June 1942, but with the defeat of the Japanese Navy in this battle, the vessel could not offload its troops, and was therefore forced to go back. The ship arrived at Guam on June 13, 1942.

With little success as an armed merchant cruiser, and with the ever increasing need for guns in other theatres of the War, the deck guns of the *Kiyosumi Maru* were removed in October 1943. On November 4, 1943, having left Truk Lagoon for Rabaul, the ship was bombed and had to be towed to the nearest port, at Kavieng. Having reached Kavieng, the *Kiyosumi Maru* was again attacked during an air raid on Christmas Day of the same year. With repairs on board having been effected, the freighter then set a return course to Truk. Having steamed approximately 400 miles, the ship was again attacked, this time by the US submarine *Balao*. Reports say that at some time after 23.00 hrs on January 1, 1944, the *Kiyosumi Maru* was hit by three torpedoes aft of the bridge. With her engine room crippled, the forward hold flooded, and at least 71 on board reported injured, the *Kiyosumi Maru* did not sink. Another vessel, the *Oyoda*, took her in tow. Two of the escort ships of this trip, the *Naka*, and *CH29*, were also destined to be sunk in Operation Hailstone.

Having arrived at Truk Lagoon without further mishap, the *Kiyosumi Maru* was allocated a position at the repair anchorage north of Fefan island. At 09.00 on February 17, the ship reportedly received a bomb hit in Number 2 hold. Later that morning, there were two hits, or very near misses either side of the bridge area. Some 43 personnel were killed, and nine seriously wounded. The *Kiyosumi Maru* sank shortly afterwards, her back finally broken.

Today the wreck lies with the bows pointing east, several hundred metres north of Fefan island, in what used to be the Japanese Repair Anchorage.

DIVING INFORMATION

LYING squarely on its port beam, the ship's name, though covered in algae, remains legible on the bow. A row of portholes lie facing upwards, and make quite a nice photograph. The port anchor is out, and the winch mechanism for both these anchors is sheltered by a large, empty gun platform. The forecastle can be entered by one of the bulkhead doors, and approximately 8m inside this passageway, there is a lantern locker, with not only many of the ship's brass and copper lanterns in a remarkable state of preservation, but also still in the alcoves of the racking system.

Number 1 hold contains much unrecognisable junk and silt, and can be entered by either the manholes on the main deck (now tilted over 90 degrees), or by the hole made from a torpedo explosion on the starboard side of Number 1 hold. The shell plating on this shallower starboard beam of the wreck is buckled from the explosion. Throughout the length of the starboard beam there are some magnificent soft and hard corals, as well as many schools of fish. Number 1 hold contains a tangle of junk, and heaps of silt. The explosion in the ship's hull has damaged the aft bulkhead to such an extent that it is now possible to swim through to Number 2 hold, but apart from a lathe, this hold appears empty.

The forward cargo winch house is located between holds 1 and 2, and is big enough to explore inside. There are two empty gun platforms either side of the holds on this foredeck.

Number 3 hold appears to have been some form of cold storage area, for there are still remains of some cork insulation for the bulkheads, as well as coiled piping

Opposite: diver over the silent propellors of a wreck.

that may have been used for cooling the hold. It is around this area that a 2m long bronze range finder can be located. This might have been an integral part of the fire control system for all of the vessel's eight guns, and would almost certainly have been located above the bridge. Why it wasn't removed with the artillery pieces is a mystery.

The superstructure was raised two decks above main deck, but three decks for the bridge. This was the area of most destruction for the ship, and though it is possible to enter and explore the cabins here, both orientation and tangled metalwork make progress very slow. The cable ties have since rotted, and left a web of drooping and sagging wires throughout this area of the ship. Finds in the lower levels have included assorted crockery, cooking utensils, and some human remains.

There are two twin-barrelled AA guns aft of the bridge, though one set has now fallen down. The large funnel carries a big brass steam whistle, as well as the very large "A" insignia of the Kokusai Kisen K.K. line.

Number 4 hold contains a couple of bicycles strapped up on the bulkhead that are in remarkable condition. There is a cargo of 45-gallon fuel oil drums, but there is also a consignment of deadly-looking depth charges. Distinctly different from the bigger fuel drums, and stored separately, these charges are the size of small dustbins. They also have regular rows of holes in their lower halves, which were to facilitate their sinking. Divers are of course advised to leave well alone.

Number 5 hold has two empty gun platforms on either side of it. Particularly interesting is the pair of torpedo launchers mounted on the port side of the ship, aft of this hold. The various hydraulic hoses, cables, and gearing, as well as the assortment of valves and gauges necessary for its operation, can all be made out.

The stern of the *Kiyosumi Maru* carries the last of the eight empty gun platforms, but worthy of a visit is the very big four-bladed propeller and rudder at 27m.

Abandoned crockery, like that found on the Kiyosumi Maru, may be seen on many of Truk's wrecks.

NAME:	The LIGHTER.
TONNAGE:	Unknown.
DIMENSIONS:	Approximately 40m in length.
SHIP TYPE:	Unknown.
SUNKEN ATTITUDE:	Upright.
DEPTH TO SEABED:	25m.
DEPTH TO WRECK:	22m (at bow) 19m (at stern).
FEATURES OF NOTE:	Artefacts in cabins.

FOUND by Dan E. Bailey in May 1972, the name, history, and purpose of this vessel remain a mystery.

DIVING INFORMATION

POINTING in a vaguely north-westerly direction, this wreck can be found just off the west coast of Uman. It can be comfortably explored on a single dive, and often turns up some interesting finds.

With the crew's quarters and messing facilities in the bow, and the bridge behind, followed by the captain's quarters, then the engine room, this wreck can be comfortably explored in a single dive. Swimming around the engine room, though, can be a little cramped at times.

Finds include a collection of 78rpm records, assorted crockery, and uniforms, as well as the ship's wheel, engine telegraph, and two large generators.

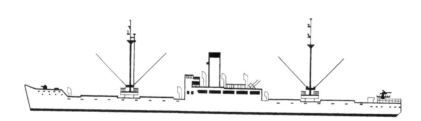

NAME:	MATSUTAN MARU.
TONNAGE:	1,999.
DIMENSIONS:	87m x 12.1m x 6.2m.
SHIP TYPE:	Type 1D cargo.
SUNKEN ATTITUDE:	Upright.
DEPTH TO SEABED:	50m.
DEPTH TO WRECK:	38m to forecastle.
FEATURES OF NOTE:	Shells, truck.

BUILT in 1942, as part of the mass production programme for shipbuilding in Japan, the *Matsutan Maru* was a standard 10 four-hold freighter. It had a single

Overleaf: the coral-covered remains of a massive deck gun.

screw driven by a 1,100ihp engine, and would cruise at speeds of around 10 knots.

This ship is thought to have been the vessel attacked during the morning of the second day of attacks, in Operation Hailstone. At least one hit was then recorded aft of the superstructure.

No positive identification has yet been made of the wreck north-east of the *Kikukawa* and *Ojima Maru*s, and south-east of the *Nagano Maru*. This unidentified shipwreck in the Fourth Fleet anchorage, west of tiny Fanamu island, and north north-east of Eten island, is believed to be that of the *Matsutan Maru*, only because it is of the same specification. The vessel was found in 1980.

DIVING INFORMATION

THE raked bow has both anchors stowed in their respective hawse pipes, but no deck gun. The piles of silt in the forecastle were not searched, but the cabin here appears to be empty.

Number 1 hold hatch cover beams remain intact, and there are two lorries stowed on the top of these. These are not in as good a condition as the lorries of the *Hoki Maru*, but worth seeing nonetheless. They are possibly Model 94 (1934) 6 x 4 trucks. They have small cranes fitted to their flatbeds. There are reports of a third lorry having fallen from the deck onto the seabed. Due to the depth here, there is not a great deal of coral growth to attract the reef diver.

Number 2 hold can be reached by swimming through from Number 1 hold, or by the main deck. This hold contains fuel oil drums, as well as artillery shells, bags of set cement, and a large compressor. It looks like a bit of a junk yard.

The midships superstructure rises only one deck above main deck level, but two decks for the bridge area. Aft of the damaged, though still standing smoke stack, are two AA gun brackets and a set of empty lifeboat davits on either side of the wreck.

Number 3 hold only contains a cargo of large fuel oil drums, while the aftmost Number 4 hold appears to be the most damaged area of the ship. Both shell plates and decking are buckled and twisted from obvious hits or near misses of the large explosions that sank the ship.

The stern castle carries a 3in deck gun on a platform, as well as the emergency steering position for the rudder.

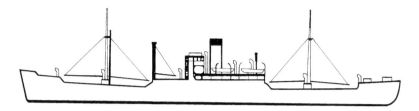

NAME:	MOMOKAWA MARU.
TONNAGE:	3,829.
DIMENSIONS:	107.5m x 15.2m x 7m.
SHIP TYPE:	Freighter-passenger.
SUNKEN ATTITUDE:	Listing heavily to port.
DEPTH TO SEABED:	40m.
DEPTH TO WRECK:	21m (to bridge).
FEATURES OF NOTE:	Trucks, and aircraft parts.

BUILT in 1940 by the Kawasaki Dockyard Co of Kobe, this five-hold freighter began service for the Kawasaki line in March 1941. It had a single screw, powered by a coal-fired turbine that generated some 2,468hp. This gave the ship a maximum speed of nearly 15 knots, and a comfortable cruising speed of 12 knots. Designed to transport timber through the iceberg-filled waters between Siberia and Japan, the *Momokawa Maru* was fitted with both strengthened bow and hull plates, as well as larger cargo derricks.

After just over two years of such service, the *Momokawa Maru* was finally requisitioned for military use on June 18, 1943. Not much is known of its eight months military service, but the vessel was sunk on the second day of Operation Hailstone. It had received a direct hit amidships from a 1,000 lb bomb.

The wreck was located on March 29, 1982 by Klaus P. Lindemann. It lies about half a mile from the east shore of Dublon, in what was the Fourth Fleet anchorage.

DIVING INFORMATION

THE bow is of the modern "rake" design, and here the diver can find the ship's name. This is characteristically written in both Japanese and English, with an ever-increasing veil of coral growing over it. The port anchor chain leads out of the hawsepipe, and down to the seabed. There is no deck gun here, so the predominant feature of this area is the windlass. A spare anchor may be found bolted to the forecastle bulkhead.

Number 1 hold contains a jumble of aviation equipment including aircraft wings, fuselage parts, aero engines, spare propellers, gas cylinders, a consignment of tyres, and the remains of a lorry. At about 39m, towards the front of this hold, there is a cargo of bombs and large artillery shells. With the tilt of the shipwreck, nearly all of this cargo has fallen over to the port side.

Number 2 hold can be reached by swimming through the 'tween deck space of Number 1 hold, or by entering from the hatch cover area. By finning through via

75

the 'tween decks, the diver will find the forward section and cockpit of a small bomber. This is either a Japanese built DC 3, or a Betty bomber. The 40-ton cargo derricks originally used for lifting huge baulks of timber, are located on the main deck between Number 1 and Number 2 hold, with the foremast. Number 2 hold itself contains more aircraft parts, as well as the remains of four more lorries. An interesting find for divers here are the large, cigar-shaped wing tanks, used for carrying fuel to increase the range of any fighter-bomber. They come complete with tail fins, which were used when the empty tank was jettisoned after use. There are reports of these fuel tanks having been used as bombs to increase the severity of any fire over a target.

Number 3 hold is raised one deck above main deck level, and located aft of the kingpost and cargo derricks used for this hold. Swimming through the hatch cover beams that remain intact, there is a cargo of fuel oil drums. Some of these unmistakably crushed by the pressure at this depth.

The midships superstructure rises only one deck further, except for the bridge area that stands two decks higher. This part of the ship remains relatively intact. Marine growth cloaks the rudderstand (or ship's helm), and the engine telegraph, but both are still attached to the deck. The ship's compass has fallen down to the port side of ship. The bridge of the *Momokawa Maru* is not as spacious as some of the other wrecks, but worth a visit nonetheless. Exploration below the bridge reveals the ship's bell, with its name in both Japanese and English. Here too, there is a fine collection of porcelain, with some pieces displaying the owner's mark. Other reported finds in this superstructure area are of a Nambu 8mm pistol, a small dinner service bell, bottles of saki, and a locker full of dinner service crockery. Aft of the bridge is the tall but damaged smoke stack, some ventilators, and sufficient davits to carry four lifeboats, two on either side of this upper boat deck. Much of the railing here is intact too. Access into the engine room can be gained by the skylights aft of the smoke stack. These are fixed in the open position.

Number 4 and Number 5 holds, with the exception of some fuel oil drums, are empty of any distinguishable cargo. The decking and hull display a considerable amount of damage here, and it is obviously the location of the bomb hit on February 18. The cargo derricks and aft mast are all appreciably larger than normal, to facilitate handling the heavy cargo of lumber that the *Momokawa Maru* was designed to carry. There were at some time two pieces of field artillery fixed to the decking here. Their wheels were apparently replaced by a fixed mount bolted to the ship's deck, one either side. Only the starboard gun remains on its metal stand, while its port side equivalent apparently lies in pieces on the seabed, perhaps under the ship's hull. One or both of these guns was in action when the vessel was sunk. This is evidenced by the number of spent shell cases in the area, along with gaps in the ammo boxes for these guns. Though covered in corals, clams, and sponges now, this starboard gun and armoured shield remain impressive.

The stern castle may be entered by some skylights in the deck. Inside this area may be found the emergency steering position, and the rudder gear. Underneath the stern is the rudder, and the large five-bladed propeller.

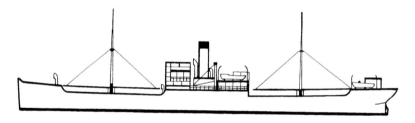

NAME:	NAGANO MARU.
TONNAGE:	3,824.
DIMENSIONS:	105.1m x 15.2m x 7.3m.
SHIP TYPE:	Freighter-passenger.
SUNKEN ATTITUDE:	Upright with 20 degree list to port.
DEPTH TO SEABED:	60-70m.
DEPTH TO WRECK:	46m (to forecastle deck).
FEATURES OF NOTE:	Anti-aircraft guns on boat deck.

BUILT in 1917 by Mitsubishi Heavy Industries, the *Nagano Maru* was a single-screw vessel, driven by a reciprocal coal-fired steam engine, and was capable of a maximum speed of 14.3 knots. During the war with China the ship was briefly requisitioned by the Japanese Army from September to 12 December, 1937, to be used as a transport. The vessel's return to civilian duties lasted only until June, 1941, when the *Nagano Maru* was again commandeered, this time by the Japanese Navy. This is likely to have been the period when the freighter was armed with its two deck guns and AA armaments. A further change of ownership came about in December 1942, when the Japanese Army took control.

Soon after 06.00 on the morning of February 17, 1944, the AA guns of the *Nagano Maru* opened up on the first wave of US fighters. The plan for this first attack of Operation Hailstone was to neutralise the airfields, and gain air superiority, but the emphasis soon shifted, and the *Nagano Maru* was attacked by the second wave. Several near misses by 500lb bombs pierced the ship's hull and fatally wounded the captain. The action caused a big explosion mistakenly believed by the US pilots to be the ship blowing up. It did, however, start several fires in the holds fore and aft. Whether the vessel sank because of the serious fires in Number 3 hold, or because her hull was ruptured by shrapnel, is not known; but the captain died at 07.35, and the crew carried everyone off at about 09.00. The *Nagano Maru* sank around 12.00 that same day.

The first recorded find of this wreck was during March 1978. She lies in the middle of what was the Fourth Fleet anchorage, east of Dublon island.

DIVING INFORMATION

THE plumb-type bow, descending straight down, is an indication of the age of this ship. The starboard anchor was apparently out at the time the *Nagano Maru* sank, for as the ship fell to the bottom, the chain for this anchor crumpled into a heap on the seabed. The bow gun and armoured shield are, surprisingly for the depth, covered in a wide variety of marine growth. The depth here is 46m, going to the seabed maximum of 60-65m. Aft of the bow gun are the twin anchor winches. There is a spare anchor bolted in the usual place on the forecastle bulkhead, and a collection of lanterns may be found inside the cabins here, plus a pair of shoes.

Number 1 and Number 2 holds, with the exception of some fuel oil drums, are empty of recognisable cargo. The hatch cover beams for these holds remain in place and it is possible to swim inside, but the increasing depth severely limits bottom time here. The foremast and cargo derrick have collapsed over to port. The substantial wooden drums which carried the coils of heavy-duty power cable near Number 2 hold, have since been burned or rotted to nothing. Another indication of the ship's age can be seen in the deck rails either side of the *Nagano Maru*, instead of the now customary and more substantial bulwarks.

The bridge rises two decks above main deck level, while the rest of the midship's superstructure remains only one deck higher. Although marine organisms have obviously eaten some of the woodwork, most of it will almost certainly have been consumed by the fire that raged on board from around 07.00 to around midday of February 17, 1944, when the ship finally sank. Because of this, the wooden partitioning and deck boards of this older ship are absent. The result is easier for the diver to swim around and explore. The ship's helm remains standing in the bridge area, although only the brass rim of the ship's wooden wheel remains. There are also two engine telegraphs to be found, but because the wooden decking has been destroyed, one of these lies on top of a deck support beam of the lower deck, while the other is hanging upside down from its chain mechanism on the port side.

The much corroded and blast-damaged smoke stack lies, like everything else, over towards port. Aft of the smoke stack can be found two sets of engine room skylights. The extreme depth of the engine-room, though, all but forbids serious exploration. The two pairs of AA guns that opened up on the first wave of US fighters can be found on this upper boat deck. What looks like three field kitchens can also be found in this area. They appear to have fire boxes set underneath large rice bowls, and each unit, being bolted to the starboard side of the deck, seems to be a fixture of the *Nagano Maru*. Below decks there are beer bottles and assorted crockery.

Number 3 hold is where the worst of the fires was started, so it should come as no surprise for the diver to find this hold empty of any recognisable cargo. Nearly all of the hatch cover beams for this hold have been blown away.

Number 4 hold carries some of its cargo of large 45-gallon drums, while further aft the sterncastle is reached. Here there is another spare anchor, as well as a very interesting steam engine, helm, and chain steering mechanism, for operating the rudder. This too betrays the age of the freighter.

The single four-bladed propeller can be seen underneath the overhanging stern, although the depth limits any real examination.

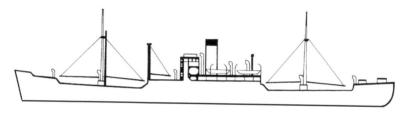

NAME:	NIPPO MARU.
TONNAGE:	3,764.
DIMENSIONS:	107.3m x 15.2m x 8.3m.
SHIP TYPE:	Cargo.
SUNKEN ATTITUDE:	Upright with 20 degree list to port.
DEPTH TO SEABED:	44-50m.
DEPTH TO WRECK:	24m (to bridge).
FEATURES OF NOTE:	Tank, trucks, field guns, interesting small cargo, and intact bridge area.

BUILT in 1936 by the Kawasaki Dockyard Company of Kobe, near Osaka, the *Nippo Maru* had a single screw, driven by two steam turbines, which could generate 500nhp.

Owned initially by Okazaki Kisen, then by Mitsubishi, the *Nippo Maru* was used to import bananas from Taiwan. The vessel was requisitioned by the Japanese Navy in August, 1941, and used as a water carrier. The metal vessels in Number 2 hold bear witness that the ship was performing just this task during February of 1944.

The *Nippo Maru* had entered Truk Lagoon on February 10 of that year with five other ships. The *Nippo Maru*, while at anchor in the Fourth Fleet anchorage east of Dublon, was attacked between 07.00-08.30 on February 17. The US fighter-bombers scored three 500lb-bomb hits around the stern of the *Nippo Maru*, but did not observe the ship sinking. Certainly it had disappeared when the *Aikoku Maru* exploded nearby two hours later.

Although the shipwreck was dived on and filmed by Jacques Cousteau's 1969 expedition, positive identification was not apparently made until June 16, 1980. The *Nippo Maru* now lies alongside a deep-water reef, with the bows pointing north.

DIVING INFORMATION

IT should be noted that unless needlessly provoked, the black-tipped reef sharks that frequent the area of this wreck, present little or no threat to the diver.

The raked bow tilts with the rest of the wreck over to port at an angle of around 20 degrees. The port anchor is out, and the forecastle deck appears relatively uncluttered. A large black tree coral sits like a figurehead on the top of the bow. There is a steel swivel mount that tapers from its wide base to where the deck gun

would have been, although the artillery piece itself is missing. Also on this deck are the big winches for lowering and raising the anchors. A spare anchor can be found bolted to the forecastle bulkhead, and the forward cabins here may be entered from a door in this bulkhead. Finds in this part of the ship include heaps of the crew's blankets, beer bottles, and stacks of rubber boots.

Number 1 hold has a lorry lying across it, with the forward wheels hanging over the port side of the ship. A second lorry can be found lying on the seabed alongside the ship's hull. It is highly likely that one lorry would have been secured on either side of this hold, but that the explosions and the sinking jolted them to their new positions. These trucks are not in as good a condition as those found on the *Hoki Maru*, but they are worth a look. The cargo inside this hold might well cause the diver to hesitate for a while, for the first objects to be seen are the large hemispherical beach mines and the equally sinister huge, brown, glass acid jars. The 106.5lb hemispherical beach mines would have held 46lbs of explosive charge. These mines would have been primed by screwing in two lead alloy horns to the top of each mine. It goes without saying that no diver should attempt to screw in any of these separately stored lead alloy horns!

The contents of the large glass acid jars could well have been destined for the various batteries used by the Japanese forces. These jars would have been carefully packed inside a wire framework which, to prevent accidental breakage, would have held a packing of straw in place around the jars. With the corks, straw and wire now rotted away, these jars serve only as curious fish tanks for hapless marine life.

Other finds in Number 1 hold include the grey clothed Model 93 Navy gas masks and filter canisters, water transfer hose, a pile of logs, artillery shells some 60cm in length, and tucked away on the port side of the hold, towards aft, several wooden boxes of small arms ammunition. A very interesting find of two bronze range finders, each approximately 1.5m long, can be seen on the 'tween deck of the aft side of this first hold, their position suggesting that they were carried as cargo, and perhaps destined for a Japanese warship. Access into the next hold can be gained below deck, as these holds are inter-connecting.

Number 2 hold does not have a great deal of space to explore, for most of this hold is taken up with possibly the ship's most valuable cargo: four square water tanks. These have obviously taken some damage, and gaps bear testimony to the fact that two such tanks floated out of this hold during or shortly after the sinking. These two tanks later sank in the shallow water of the reef to the west. Also in this hold, stored in the forward part, are neatly stacked rows of 10cm artillery shells. The warheads are stored separately in boxes. Again, access into the next hold aft can be made underneath the decking, for these holds are connected by passageways down either side of the ship.

Sitting on the port side of the main deck, facing forward, is a Japanese Type 95 Ha-Go light tank. These were made in large numbers from 1935 onwards. As was apparently usual for the time, this tank was not being transported with its 37mm main gun mounted. These light tanks had a crew of three men, and were powered

Opposite: engine telegraph on
the bridge of the Nippo Maru.

by a 6 cylinder in-line air cooled diesel engine. This could generate between 110-240hp depending on the rpm of the engine. They weighed 10 tons, and were 4.6m long, 2m wide, and 2.1m high. Each tank was capable of carrying 130 rounds for the main gun, as well as 2,970 rounds of 7.7mm ammunition, for the hull-mounted machine gun.

Number 3 hold follows the classic lines of the five-hold freighters of this period, and is raised one deck above its forward and aft counterparts. Lying against the superstructure, at the starboard aft end of this hold, there is an AA machine gun with belts of ready ammunition. Several artillery shells, and the large derrick that would have lowered or raised the cargo into or out of this smaller hold, now lie on the deck. This would have originally been mounted and operated from the kingpost at the hold's forward edge. There is a great deal of silt heaped up inside this hold, but the diver will find a multitude of assorted bottles here. Descending to the lowest 'tween deck of this hold, the diver will find a collection of infantry mess tins, a consignment of boots, more bottles, many and various galley stores. It is possible to continue aft from this hold, and swim underneath the superstructure to the coal bunkers near the engine room.

The midships superstructure and bridge are among the most impressive in Truk. Relatively devoid of marine growth, the overall appearance suggests a more recent sinking than other wrecks in the lagoon. The depth to the top of the superstructure is 24m. The bridge area is possibly the most complete of any of the known shipwrecks in the lagoon. Immediately apparent upon entry through either the windows or the doors of the bridge are the engine telegraph, and the equally intact rudderstand with compass. The wood of the ship's wheel has been eaten away, but the brass rim still hangs from the wheelhub it once turned. At the back of the bridge there is at least one decorative sake cup, and a ship's strong box – one of three to be found on the *Nippo Maru*. One or all of these contained some valuable codes and ciphers that the Japanese reported lost with the *Nippo Maru*. The cavernous darkness of this all-but intact bridge area frequently plays host to a myriad tiny fish fry, or opal sweepers. Although a flashgun is a prerequisite of photography in here, this part of the ship is really photogenic.

Aft of the bridge area, there is the tall funnel, the remains of the ventilators, the four sets of lifeboat davits, and the half closed engine room skylights. Due to the restricted opening, these skylights should not be depended upon for access into, or egress from, the engine room. Descending below this boat deck, to the cabins underneath, the diver will find the ship's galley on the starboard side. A large coal fired stove dominates this room, with many oriental style cooking bowls, implements, and cutlery to be found lying around, or hung up on the aft bulkhead. Photographers should plan to be the first inside here, if the silt is not to ruin any photographs. Forward of the galley, the absence of doors suggests that these were made of wood, and that they have since been eaten away. The finds here are almost innumerable, and it seems every diver discovers something else. Uniform buttons, phonographic records, a metal box of precision navigational instruments, binoculars, two sets of reindeer antlers, teapots, sake and beer bottles, rice dishes, sake cups, brass lanterns, radio equipment, even crockery bearing the twin blue striped flag symbol of the Nippoh Kaiun K.K. shipping line – all can be found by the discerning diver. Dive guides prove invaluable on a wreck such as the *Nippo Maru*, for each has his secret cache of interesting or valuable artefacts. These are kept hidden by the guides to deter unscrupulous divers.

Swimming forward past the ship's head and bathroom on the port side, the diver will arrive at a doorway set into the port side of the engine room casing. There is a second doorway into this area, and this is found one deck above. As might be expected, this engine room casing occupies the central part of the super-structure, around which all of the various cabins and other rooms are positioned. As the diver swims through either of these doors, the engine room drops to a depth of around 40m. Catwalks, gantries, gratings, valves, pipework and gauges fill this more roomy part of the ship.

Number 4 hold is where the diver will find three Japanese Model 1 (1941) 47mm field guns. These are lying on the main deck, at a depth of 32m, to star-board of this hold. These anti-tank guns weighed 1,600 lbs, had a muzzle velocity of 2,700 fps, and fired either armour-piercing high explosive, or standard high explosive rounds. The white-walled tyres seem strangely unaffected by the water pressure here, and that is because they were sponge filled. The armour-plated deflection shield of these guns now look like impromptu picnic tables, as divers have brought up various finds of crockery to study from the greater depths below. The depth here is 32m. There is a theory that these guns were originally mounted on the conical metal pivot points that can also be found nearby on this deck.

Swimming inside Number 4 hold, the diver will find many bottles, and assorted

Anti-aircraft guns (with scattered crockery) on the Nippo Maru.

items of crockery. Here too there is evidence of the explosions that sank the *Nippo Maru*. The port side of the hull here has been blown open, and the twisted metal-work is evidence of one of the three 500lb bombs that sent this ship to the bottom. The starboard side of this hold contains the remains of two carts, six hospital beds, and many old style batteries.

The aft mast, some steel cabling, ventilator remains and the cargo derricks for the two aft holds are located between holds 4 and 5.

Number 5 hold contains gun barrels, and seven metal mountings each complete with gears and turning wheel that were probably meant to go with the guns. As well as these, there are coils of electrical cable, telephone wiring, and barbed wire. A cart, and rows of gunpowder canisters may also be found here. Down on the starboard side there are rows of cement bags that have long since set. Stowed up on the main deck, to starboard of this hold, are two 5m-long gun barrels. This cargo seems to suggest the guns were destined for fixed emplacements, and the steel concrete reinforcing rods stowed on main deck just aft of this hold would back this up.

The sterncastle, like the forecastle, has a gun platform, but no gun. There is another spare anchor bolted to the bulkhead, and access into the aft cabins can be made by either the starboard or port doorway of this bulkhead. Divers could then exit from the sterncastle skylight which has disappeared either from the explosions of February 17, 1944, or by corrosion. Of interest here is the steering mechanism for the rudder. This takes the form of a big electric motor, gearbox, and other pieces of machinery.

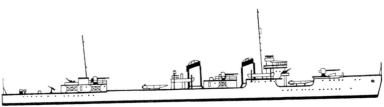

NAME:	The OITE.
TONNAGE:	1,400 (displacement).
DIMENSIONS:	99.6m x 9.1m x 2.9m.
SHIP TYPE:	Destroyer (Kamikaze Class).
SUNKEN ATTITUDE:	Broken in two. Stern is upright.
DEPTH TO SEABED:	61-67m.
DEPTH TO WRECK:	55m to stern structures.
FEATURES OF NOTE:	None.

BUILT in 1924 by the Uraga Dock Company Ltd of Tokyo, this Kamikaze Class destroyer represented an improvement on the earlier Minekaze Class. This destroyer "Number 11" was renamed the *Oite* four years later. It was armed with four depth charge throwers, 18 depth charges, two twin 21in torpedo launchers, three 4.7in deck guns, between six and ten 25mm AA guns, and two 7.7mm machine guns. Its Parsons geared turbines could generate 38,500hp at the twin shafts, and drive the warship a maximum of 37.3 knots.

Following the US photographic overflight of Truk Lagoon on February 4, 1944, Admiral Koga correctly judged that the lagoon was about to be attacked. He ordered most warships of the Japanese Combined Fleet to sail, and the *Oite* left Truk Lagoon with the light cruiser *Agano* on February 15. This was to be the last voyage of Oite's captain Uono, who was scheduled to take up a naval staff position on his return to Japan. Historians disagree about the exact location and details of the attack, but somewhere between 160-200 miles north west of Truk, while enroute to Japan via Saipan, the cruiser *Agano* was attacked by a submarine. The ship began to list, and while the Japanese *Subchaser 28* was able to take on some of the survivors, it was left to the destroyer *Oite* to take on 450 men and the *Agano*'s captain. The *Agano* sank the following day. The *Oite* then set sail with *Subchaser 28* for Saipan, over 450 miles to the north west.

At 16.00 on February 17, the two vessels were ordered back to assist shipping in Truk Lagoon. By now Operation Hailstone was well advanced. The *Oite* arrived at Truk in the early hours of the following day, and was reported by US pilots to be near the north pass at 06.55. At about the same time, the naval gunnery officer in charge of defence of this pass sent a radio message to the *Oite* asking why they were entering the lagoon during an attack. The *Oite* captain replied that he was following orders, and shortly after this received another radio message, this time from Truk HQ – that he was to head for Saipan at once. The captain then replied "I am already inside the lagoon."

Very soon after this exchange, the *Oite* came under heavy straffing fire from US fighters. With a ship's complement of 148 men, and over 450 survivors of the Agano, there were many casualties. One of the first sweeps raked the bridge, and killed the captain of the ship, Lt Commander Uono. Command was then assumed by the *Agano*'s gunnery officer, and when he was killed, the captain of the Agano took command. A fire had started near the second funnel, and when five Avenger planes attacked, one of their torpedoes hit and the *Oite* blew up and sank immediately. With over 598 men on board, only 20 survived.

The wreckage was found on March 1, 1986, by Japanese researcher Tomoyuki Yoshimura, Gradvin Aisek of Truk's Blue Lagoon Dive Shop, and a local man who had seen droplets of oil on the sea.

DIVING INFORMATION

THE wreckage is in two parts, and in very deep water. The forward section lies upside down, with the bridge firmly jammed into the sand. Various pieces of assorted crockery may be found in the cabins around here.

There is a gap of around 12m, then the diver will come across the upright stern section of the ship. The shallowest part of the wreck may be found here, but even

Overleaf: diver over a tank
on the San Francisco Maru.

at 54m, this is deeper than most sport divers would care to go. There is a raised 4.7in deck gun in this stern area, and one pair of AA guns to be found in front and behind it.

With the loss of 570 lives on such a small vessel, it should come as no surprise that there are hundreds of human remains strewn around the decks, cabins, and seabed.

Only by diving with mixed gases will the diver be able to carry out any real exploration of this destroyer. Blue Lagoon Dive Shop is the only Truk diving out-fit to take divers on this wreck. Even then, these extremely experienced divers must be satisfied with the customer diver's experience at depth before they will agree to take him.

NAME:	The OJIMA.
TONNAGE:	800 (displacement).
DIMENSIONS:	48.9m x 9.5m x 3.4m.
SHIP TYPE:	Salvage tug (Tategami Class).
SUNKEN ATTITUDE:	Broken in two. Foreship lies on starboard side.
DEPTH TO SEABED:	36m & 46m.
DEPTH TO WRECK:	24m & 40m.
FEATURES OF NOTE:	Landing craft nearby.

BUILT in 1940 by Maizuru Kaigun Kosho, 90km north of Osaka, the *Ojima* was a Tategami Class salvage tug. It was armed with two 25mm AA guns, and six depth charges. It was equipped with three 5-ton and one 10-ton derrick, salvage pumps and compressors. Its twin screws were powered by two reciprocating vertical expansion engines, generating some 2,200ihp.

Both the *Ojima* and the *Kikukawa Maru* were sunk by the same explosion on October 7, 1943. Three landing craft, and a small tug were also destroyed with all hands. The *Ojima* had been sent to assist with fire fighting operations on board the *Kikukawa Maru*, and had apparently tied up alongside the freighter. The *Ojima*, like the other smaller vessels, was operating sea pumps to feed water to the fire-fighting teams on the freighter. With so much shipping sunk during Operation Hailstone and other bombing raids, it must be remembered there were "normal" accidents in these anchorages. The fire on board the *Kikukawa Maru*, and the resulting explosion that destroyed both this and the *Ojima*, as well as a few other little boats, was one of these accidents. The explosion killed around 50 men.

The wreck lies in what was the Fourth Fleet anchorage, east of Eten island. It is only 60-80m north-east of the *Kikukawa Maru*.

DIVING INFORMATION

THE bow section of this wreck lies in 36m of water. The port anchor is housed, but the starboard anchor is out. This portion of the wreck lies on its starboard beam. Holds 1 and 2 are located fore and aft of the mast repectively, but aft of Number 2 hold the tug is broken off.

Swimming down, and approximately 60m to the south-east, the diver will find the other half of this vessel. At a greater depth of between 42-45m, this aft part of the wreck contains the superstructure and tug's stern.

Between the two parts of this wreck, and to the north, in 39m of water, it is possible to find a Daihatsu landing craft that was also involved in the fatal explosion. Pointing south, and about 18m long, this craft is in excellent condition, and shows no apparent damage from the blast that sank it.

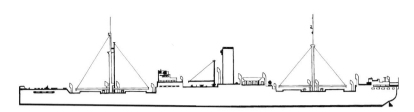

NAME: REIYO MARU.
TONNAGE: 5,446.
DIMENSIONS: 135.3m x 16.2m x 8.9m.
SHIP TYPE: Freighter-transport.
SUNKEN ATTITUDE: Upright on even keel.
DEPTH TO SEABED: 65m.
DEPTH TO WRECK: 53m to deck.
FEATURES OF NOTE: Damaged bridge area.

BUILT in 1920, by Asano Sanbashi Co, of Tsurumi, in Yokohama, this five-hold freighter had a complement of 48 men. It also had facilities to accommodate four passengers. The ship has a single screw, and could attain a maximum of 14 knots. Commandeered by first the Imperial Japanese Army, on October 10, 1941; then the Japanese Navy, from November 17, 1943, the *Reiyo Maru* was used as a military transport ship during the war. It seems likely it was the vessel sunk by two direct hits from US dive-bombers, during the first morning of attacks on February 17, 1944. These 1,000lb bombs reportedly exploded aft of the bridge, and amidships.

The wreck was first located in 1973, but being so infrequently dived, it was subsequently lost, and found again in 1980. The *Reiyo Maru* lies pointing in a north-east direction, and remains a relatively undived wrecksite because of the great depth it lies in. Currently beyond the safe limit of compressed air sport diving, it might be visited more frequently with the increasing poularity of mixed gas diving.

DIVING INFORMATION

THE bow is of the older "plumb" type, with no visible rake to it at all. Both anchors are paid out, and accumulated anchor chain is found on the seabed. At a depth of 49m, the deck of the forecastle has no gun platform, or deck gun. The anchor windlass, though, is very prominent here.

Number 1 hold contains only a few fuel oil drums, but the depth here, as with all the holds, prevents any serious exploration inside. Between this and Number 2 hold is the winch mechanism for the cargo derricks, as well as the remains of the foremast, which has fallen aft and to port. The very distinctive triangular shaped crosstrees, located halfway up both the fore and aft masts, were a major factor in the identification of the *Reiyo Maru*.

Number 2 hold has some cargo of railway track lengths.

The midships superstructure did rise three decks above main deck, but there is a great deal of damage from at least one explosion aft of the bridge, as well as from the foremast that came crashing down on the port side of the bridge.

Number 3 hold, behind the bridge and deck cabins, is appreciably smaller than the other four, and appears to be empty. Another sign of the fatal blasts in this area is the split in the starboard shell plating. The derricks for this hold were mounted on the kingpost, which remains standing at the aft edge of the hold. On either side of this can be found two ventilator cowls used for supplying fresh air below decks.

The tall, slim, smoke stack is one characteristic of all coal-burning steamers of this time. Incredibly though, bearing in mind the very clear and extensive bomb damage port of the smoke stack, it is still standing. Coal has poured out of the damaged hull here, and has heaped up onto the seabed. Access into the engine room can be made from the open skylights aft of the smoke stack. However, due to the damage of the explosion inside here, and the extreme depth, this is not recommended.

Moving further aft, the lifeboat davits and deck cabins can be located. Aft of these, Number 4 hold is intact, but the broken aft mast, and Number 5 hold show clear damage from some form of exploding ordnance. It is difficult to imagine that just one bomb caused all this twisted steel work, which extends right down the port side, to the sterncastle. The evidence seems to suggest that the *Reiyo Maru* was hit by at least two bombs on the port quarter, as well as one on port side amidships.

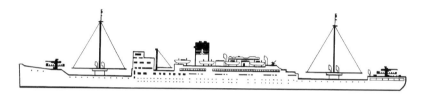

NAME:	RIO DE JANEIRO MARU.
TONNAGE:	9,626.
DIMENSIONS:	137.1m x 18.9m x 7.9m.
SHIP TYPE:	Passenger liner converted to transport.
SUNKEN ATTITUDE:	Lies on starboard side.
DEPTH TO SEABED:	40m (at bow).
DEPTH TO WRECK:	12-15m (port beam).
FEATURES OF NOTE:	Deck guns, propellers, marine life.

BUILT in 1929 by Mitsubishi Zosensho of Nagasaki, the *Rio De Janeiro Maru* was a five hold passenger-freighter. It was driven by two six cylinder Mitsubishi Sultzer Diesel engines, generating some 1,503nhp. These, and the twin screws were capable of giving the ship a maximum speed of 17.6 knots. Part of a modernisation programme, this was just one of five new ships for the Osaka Shozen Kaisha line. The ships sailed with emigrants from Japan to Hong Kong, Singapore and South Africa, then on to South America. The *Rio De Janeiro Maru* had berths for 60 first-class passengers, and 1,076 third-class passengers. Much of the accommodation was in the form of bunks, with the wider, lower, bunks being customarily used for mothers and their children. The third-class bunks were so designed that any unbooked berths on the return journey would simply be folded up to make space for cargo.

Facilities on board included five baths, eight washrooms, three sick bays, two quarantine cabins, refrigeration units, electrically-powered fresh air ventilators, and (to comply with the increased safety requirements imposed by Lloyds of London) 22 lifeboats

After just over 10 years of such service, the *Rio De Janeiro Maru* was requisitioned by the Japanese Navy on October 8, 1940. The ship was armed with two 6in guns, and AA guns, and was also given the protection of degaussing coils. This is a thick copper wire that is wound several times around the ship's hull. An electric current is then passed through this to neutralise the ship's magnetic field, that would otherwise trigger magnetic mines. This degaussing coil can still be seen over much of its length on the hull.

After the refit, the *Rio De Janeiro Maru* was attached to the Combined Fleet. Along with the light cruiser *Yura*, and six submarines, the *Rio De Janeiro Maru* made up the 5th Submarine Squadron of the 1st Battle Fleet. Her role as a submarine tender continued with a further posting, this time with the 30th Submarine Squadron. Operating from Penang in Malaya, the ship was supplying and servic-

ing submarines that were attacking Allied shipping in the Indian Ocean. The *Rio De Janeiro Maru* was apparently attacked by the US submarine *Spearfish* on July 27, 1942, while 95 miles east of Camranh, French Indochina. The ship sustained some damage, but this was repaired in Hong Kong. On April 15, 1943, the *Rio De Janeiro Maru* was reassigned as a transport, and based in Truk. With her cargo of old-style guns, it is almost certain the vessel was involved in some form of fortification programme.

The *Rio De Janeiro Maru* was attacked and bombed around midday of the first day of Operation Hailstone. It remained afloat for around 12 hours, finally sinking at 00.30 that night.

DIVING INFORMATION

THE bow lies right over on its starboard side. Both anchors are out, with the starboard anchor chain leading off about 40m into the distance. Though covered in coral now, the ship's name, or rather some of the characters that make up the name, can be made out on the port side, which faces up. As with nearly all of the ship's names, the English name is repeated below the Japanese characters. A very big bow gun may also be seen on its platform on the forecastle. The barrel is about 4.5m long, and has a 6in bore. It has swivelled around, and now points over the starboard side to the seabed below. The decking and bulkheads aft of this gun are torn and twisted to an ever-increasing extent towards the centre of what must have been several explosions, or one major one. This damage was apparently caused by the detonation of some of the bow gun ammunition, which was stored inside the forecastle, one deck below. Divers here can find brass shell cases that have opened up like blooming spring flowers.

Number 1 hold contains evidence for the explosion in the forecastle, for here there is a great deal of burned material. There was obviously a serious fire in this part of the ship. A few large artillery shells can also be found here. Between Numbers 1 and 2 holds there is a large mast house with passageways down both the port and starboard sides of the ship. These passageways are wide enough to swim along. The mast is intact, and here too are the cargo derricks that would have served the holds fore and aft of this fore mast.

Number 2 hold contains the remains of an interesting gun turret with recoil springs, turning and elevation gears. The two barrels destined for this old-style turret can also be found in this hold. Other cargo here is mainly coal. This would have contributed to the fire that has apparently burned away the liner's wooden deck boards in this forward part of the ship.

Midships superstructure can be entered and explored easily, though the silt inside is very thick in places. Because the ship is lying on its port beam, everything has fallen across the decks to the port side. Even the bridge is empty of the usual engine telegraph and rudder stand. Everything has fallen across to port, and now lies in silt and muck. A search of the cabins below and aft of the bridge will yield many stacks of china, and a few galley utensils. It is a good idea to plan the dive so that it ends in this midship region, for at the shallower depths of around

Opposite: diver entering companionway, Rio de Janeiro Maru.

12-15m, the starboard beam yields some interesting finds. Among these are the large starboard running light, located on the bridge wing, the degaussing coils wrapped around the vessel, and the long boarding ladder.

Number 3 hold is located aft of the bridge, and forward of the funnel. This is a much smaller hold to its counterparts fore and aft. Finds in here have included some ornately decorated sake bottles, beer bottles, and assorted crockery.

The funnel for the *Rio De Janeiro* supports a great deal of onion skin algae, but is an interesting feature of the old liner, for it also has a large steam whistle, steam condenser, running light, and ladder. Peering into the top of this very big feature of the ship, the diver will also see the rain deflection plates needed to protect the fires in the engine room below. Also of interest are the raised stack markings of the ship's owner, Osaka Shosen Kaisha.

A bomb hit aft of the funnel has severely damaged the starboard side of the aft superstructure, as well as Number 4 hold. Deck support beams, bulkheads, shell plating: all of these on the starboard side show considerable damage here. With so much damage to the hull, it seems strange the *Rio De Janeiro Maru* did not sink until after midnight.

Number 4 hold contains mostly coal. There is a third gun barrel similar to those in Number 2 hold. The remains of another turret mechanism can also be found here.

Number 5 hold follows behind the aft mast house which is as substantial as its forward counterpart. This last hold contains many bottles, the remains of their wooden crates, and a few fuel-oil drums.

The stern castle contains the crew's cabins, and another 6in gun mounted on the poop. At the seabed depth of 34m here, there are some big shells to be found. Also in this stern area is the auxiliary engine telegraph, which has fallen from its mounting on the deck. When swimming around the stern or over the port rails, and descending to 24m, the diver will find the two very big propellers and rudder intact. The ship's name in both Japanese and English is to be found quite legible on the stern.

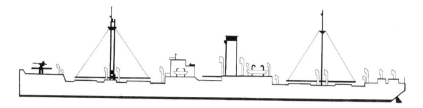

NAME:	SAN FRANCISCO MARU.
TONNAGE:	5,831 tons.
DIMENSIONS:	117.3m x 15.5m x 10.9m.
SHIP TYPE:	Passenger-cargo.
SUNKEN ATTITUDE:	Upright on a fairly even keel.
DEPTH TO SEABED:	64-73m.
DEPTH TO WRECK:	42m (to bridge) 52m (to stern).
FEATURES OF NOTE:	Three light tanks, lorries, steam-roller, shells, mines, depth charges and torpedoes.

BUILT by Kawasaki Dockyard Company, the *San Francisco Maru* was launched on March 1, 1919. With the classic lines of the old five-hold freighters, its engine could generate a maximum of 3,946hp, giving the ship a maximum speed of 14.2 knots.

Little is known of the ship's war record, but the *San Francisco Maru* was attacked by planes while working at Wewak in New Guinea, on May 4, 1943. It is next mentioned as part of a convoy of Japanese ships to Truk Lagoon. The convoy arrived on February 5, 1944, and with the threat of an American attack almost imminent, left on February 12. For some reason the *San Francisco Maru* did not leave with the convoy.

While at anchor in the Fourth Fleet anchorage east of Eten island, it seems the ship was attacked several times throughout Operation Hailstone. Finally, after fires started during the first day of air attacks, the vessel was reported to have received no fewer than six 500lb bomb hits during the afternoon of the February 18. When the initial smoke and water spray had subsided, the ship was reported to be burning furiously and sinking by the stern.

Found by Sam Redford in 1972, this wreck has since been dubbed the "Million Dollar Wreck", because of the sheer quantity and quality of cargo it holds. It remains though a special attraction for some of the local fishermen, who, despite the risk of police patrols, steal some of the old beach mines in the cargo holds. The explosive charge in these waterproof cases is then illegally used for dynamite fishing on the outer reefs of Truk Lagoon.

DIVING INFORMATION

THE bow has no rake as it is of the old plumb design. Being over 25 years old, the entire ship carries many features characteristic of the older vessels. The port anchor chain leads out of its hawse pipe, and now forms a vague "U" shape on the seabed. This line drawn by the anchor chain shows how the ship sank by the stern, then as the bows caught up and overtook the stern, the vessel moved forward before finally hitting the seabed. A small heap of chain under the bow testifies that the ship dropped straight down in the last few seconds of its sinking. The 10cm deck gun sits on top of the gun platform on the forecastle deck, and because of the limited coral growth at this depth, has not been disfigured or mishapen by layers of sessile marine life. All working parts of this artillery piece can be made out, and for this reason, the gun is classed as one of the ship's most photogenic subjects. Aft of the gun, there is a spare anchor bolted to the port side of the deck. Continuing aft, the diver will locate a second spare anchor mounted on the bulkhead.

Number 1 hold is full, almost to the brim, with hemispherical beach mines. These are Model 96 (1936) 106.5lb mines with 46lb of explosive charge. The explosives contained in this hold should be considered to be still active, and divers are therefore recommended to treat this cargo with the utmost respect. The anchors of any good dive boats tend to be lowered down to this wreck, for obvious reasons. Theft by local dynamite fishermen explains the odd gap in the neat rows of these mines. Also in this hold are the boxes of lead alloy horns used to detonate the mines. So full is this hold with mines that access into the lower 'tween decks is denied. The foremast is located aft of this first hold, although the old-style wooden cargo derricks have since rotted away. One of the steel tips of these derricks reportedly lies along the port side of Number 2 hold. It still supposedly has its steel ring, and remains of the wooden spar inside.

Number 2 hold and the surrounding area is where divers will find three Type 95 Ha-Go tanks. These Japanese light tanks were made in large numbers from 1935 onwards. They had a crew of three men, and were powered by a 6-cylinder in-line air-cooled diesel engine. This could generate between 110-240hp. The driver could attain a maximum of 28mph, and had the use of four forward gears, and one reverse. The vehicles weighed 10 tons, and were 4.6m long, 2m wide, and 2.1m high. There was usually a ground clearance of 39cm, but the suspension on these tanks has dropped. Each tank was capable of carrying 130 rounds for its 37mm model 94 main gun, as well as 2,970 rounds of 7.7mm ammunition for the hull-mounted machine gun. The armour plating varied between 6-12mm thickness. All three tanks can be seen on the main deck on either side of this hold. For safe trim of the ship, there would have been two heavy vehicles on each side. There are two tanks on starboard, one on port, and the fourth vehicle, a large steamroller, can be seen lying on the seabed off the port side. The extreme depth of the seabed here precludes any real investigation of the steamroller, which now lies on its side in 73m. From its present position, on the seabed aft of the bridge area, the steamroller evidently fell while the ship was sinking, but before the *San Francisco Maru* actually moved bow forward and hit the seabed.

Number 2 hold itself contains more extremely interesting vehicles, which remain on the hatch beams of the first 'tween deck. These are: two fuel or water

Opposite: Japanese staff car, San Francisco Maru.

tankers, one characteristically thin-barrelled high velocity 20mm anti-aircraft gun (mounted on a carriage with four small wheels), and some form of staff car. Though space in this lower deck is limited, all these vehicles make superb subjects for photography. The confined conditions and depth of 52m present very real challenges for the photographer. Descending one deck further, to the second 'tween deck below the road tankers, the diver will find many 50lb bombs stored with their tailfins uppermost. Aft of these bombs in the same hold is a radial engine for an aircraft. Other reported finds at this greater depth are boxes of 3in artillery shells, that may have been used in the deck gun.

The bridge area is to be found aft of this second hold, and rising two decks above main deck level. The bridge, like the rest of the superstructure, contained a great deal of wood in its construction, and because of fire, or wood-eating organisms, almost none is left. The cabins inside this superstructure contain many pieces of crockery, at least two glass decanters, and many beer bottles. Some of this vast collection of artefacts has been collected by previous divers, and carefully placed into a large box. Also of interest in this cabin area are the two baths towards the aft end of the superstructure. The ship's bell used to be a major attraction for photographers and divers alike, but an unscrupulous diver has since stolen this, thus depriving future visitors of the thrill in finding it.

Number 3 hold is appreciably smaller than the other four, and is located aft of the bridge, but forward of where the slim smoke stack used to be. It contains a great deal of silt, and some of the coal used for the ship's steam engine. The smoke stack was little more than a rudimentary flue. For this reason it was easily damaged by the engine boilers exploding as sea water got in. Evidence of this can be found when looking down the port side of the ship's hull. A jagged hole, with plates bent outward, just 3m below main deck level, bears witness to a sizeable internal explosion in the engine room. The boat deck aft of where the smoke stack was contains two rows of open skylights for the engine room, and a pair of ventilators with cowls intact.

Number 4 hold hatch cover beams are all but missing at main deck level. This hold contains the remains of two lorries, which lie on the hatch beams across the first 'tween deck. The lorries aside, an impressive sight for any diver in this hold is the sheer number of artillery shells stored in boxes, on both port and starboard sides. The rounds of ammunition appear to come in just two sizes. These are 3in shells stored in boxes of nine, and the slightly larger 4in shells stored in crates of ten. Because of the fact that these ammo boxes have been stacked right up to the deckhead, or ceiling, the best place to examine them is on the port side of the hold, where many of the boxes were shaken loose by the bomb hit. They make sinister but statisfying photographs. As with their forward counterparts, the mast and cargo derricks here are located between the two holds. And again, the wooden cargo derricks have burned or rotted away.

Number 5 hold contains many torpedoes, in various states of stowage. It contains torpedo parts, and a great many torpedo bodies. The high-pressure air tanks of some of these torpedoes have exploded during the rotting of their metal cases.

Some torpedoes have also ended up on the main deck. Whereas the port side of this hold has been severely damaged by the bomb explosion of the attacking aircraft, both the cargo and the ship's structure of the starboard 'tween decks remain intact. In this part of the shipwreck the diver will find an equally deadly cargo of depth charges. These remain neatly stored on deck amongst the similar, but quite distinguishable drums of fuel oil.

This stern part of the ship was hit by the bomb on February 17, 1944. Because of this hit or very near miss, the port side decking, steel supports, and hull plating were twisted, buckled and bent. The very severe damage sustained by this bomb blast can be seen by making a short excursion over the port rails of the ship, and aft of this last hold. The hull plating here is buckled, and there is a long vertical split in the ship's side. This 5m gash would have certainly been enough to cause the demise of the *San Francisco Maru*.

The sterncastle is of the very low design used at the time for this type of ship, and the diver will find only three deck cabins here. There is no deck gun at the stern. The older design of this freighter can further be noticed in the deck rails that surround the poop. Due to the excessive depth, the ship's propeller and rudder have not been examined.

Number 2 hold of the San Francisco Maru contains three type 95 Ha-Go tanks.

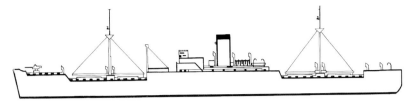

NAME:	SANKISAN MARU.
TONNAGE:	4,776 tons.
DIMENSIONS:	112m x 15.7m x 8.9m.
SHIP TYPE:	Freighter.
SUNKEN ATTITUDE:	Upright on sloping seabed.
DEPTH TO SEABED:	24m (at bow) 52m (at stern)
DEPTH TO WRECK:	12m (at bow) 46m (at stern)
FEATURES OF NOTE:	Trucks on main deck of foreship.
	Ammunition in Number 1 Hold.

BUILT in the latter part of 1941 by Harima Dockyard near Osaka, the *Sankisan Maru* was launched on January 29, 1942. Its single coal turbine engine generated some 2846 hp and was capable of driving the vessel up to a maximum noted speed of 15.8 knots.

The ship's brief civilian duties with the Kaburagi Kisen line ended with its requisition by the Japanese Navy in October 1943.

The *Sankisan* received at least one hit during the early hours of February 18, 1944. Judging from the extensive damage to the aft ship, it is widely believed that a fire started by this bomb was then responsible for detonating the cargo of ordnance stowed in the aft holds. The vessel then sank as a result of this larger explosion, and can be found off the south-west coast of Uman.

DIVING INFORMATION

THE bow is the shallowest part of the wreck at 24m. Evidently the starboard anchor was out at the time of the sinking, for this now lies underneath the heap of chain that collected as the *Sankisan* sank. There is no deck gun mounted on the forecastle, but a large windlass and a winch for each anchor may be found here. The cabin underneath this deck is worth a visit to see the ship's lanterns still stowed here. Aft of the forecastle, and stowed on the main deck, the diver will find three Japanese lorries. Two of these are to be found facing each other on the port side, abeam Number 1 hold, while the third is located on the starboard side. This starboard lorry lies diagonally across the deck, with its two front wheels turned slightly to the right. Much of the bodywork of these vehicles has rotted, but the more substantial parts remain. These include what appears to be a large tool box on one. The first lorry on the port side lies on its right side, and is not as intact as the truck on the starboard side. This starboard truck, possibly a Model 1 Toyoda 4x2 (1941), is worth photographing.

Number 1 hold itself contains a fine but apparently diminishing collection of small arms ammunition (thanks to souvenir pilfering by divers). Some of the ammo is stored in wooden crates and boxes, while thousands of loose rounds lie strewn across the deck. There is very little coral growth here, and the wood has not been eaten away. This is characteristic of nearly all the ammunition cargo found underwater, and is evidence of the slightly corrosive quality of the materials used. There are thousands of loose rounds of 7.7mm ammunition, as well as five-round clips, destined for the magazines of the Japanese Arisaka infantry rifle. Longer clips of 30 rounds may also be seen, and these were for use with the tripod mounted Model 92 (1932) heavy machine gun-anti-aircraft weapon. This ammunition was obviously destined to be used by Truk's Japanese garrison in the land battle that never took place. As well as the rifle and machine gun ammunition, there are artillery shells and boxes of detonators which are extremely dangerous, and should be treated accordingly.

The foremast, cargo winches and derricks are to be found between the first two holds. The mast house also has four ventilator stacks, although their swivelling scoops have fallen or been blown from their original positions. Inside this small mast house the diver will find hundreds of bottles, tins, and other assorted cans.

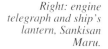

Right: engine telegraph and ship's lantern, Sankisan Maru.

The upper part of the foremast now plays host to a plethora of soft and hard corals. Sessile marine life is layered on so thick as to completely hide the mast itself, which actually breaks the surface at low tide. This part of the ship therefore makes an ideal shallower end to any dive on the wreck.

Number 2 hold is easy to enter, but at main deck level the diver will notice a long, jagged piece of metal. This is in fact a large section of the aft ship, which was blown over the superstructure in the explosion that sank the ship. The hold itself contains aeroplane engines and cowlings, five more lorries, and what may be glider fuselages.

Two lorries can be found on the port side of the ship, sitting on the first 'tween deck towards the front of this hold. The foremost truck points forward, while the vehicle behind it faces aft. A large compressor is also to be found with these aged lorries. Another lorry may be found on the aft side of this hold, again sitting on the first 'tween deck. This lorry is a little harder to get to because of the debris and silt that clutters this part of the hold, but is more intact than the other vehicles on board. There is also a lorry on the starboard side of this 'tween deck, along with two radial aero engines. Several engine cowlings may also be found near these radial engines. The second and deeper 'tween deck carries a great deal of silt at the aft edge of the hold. A careful swim between this heap of silt and the deckhead of the first 'tween deck above reveals a larger space on the other side. Around two dozen fuselages may be seen here, and their old canvas-covered wooden rib construction is very clear. There is even a flight control stick in the cockpit of some of these.

Number 3 hold can be easily entered from main deck level, which lies at a depth of 15m. This hold is not separated from Number 2 hold by a bulkhead, so the diver may choose to swim underneath the decks to gain access. This hold contains a great deal of coal for the ship's engine, and may well contain some depth charges. Most of this last cargo was removed in the early seventies, but it is known that some of this ordnance remains. Again the diver need not ascend out of the hold in order to explore the midships superstructure. The bulkheads separating the cabins from this hold were blown apart during the explosion of the aft cargo. This impromptu method of entry is safe, because the gaps are large enough to swim easily through, and there is plenty of available light in the cabins on the other side.

The midships superstructure rises one deck above Number 3 hold, but two decks for the bridge. This part of the ship was severely damaged in the explosion, particularly on the starboard side. This damage allows a great deal of light into the wreck, and makes swimming around the cabins a little easier. Access to the engine room is very difficult, and consequently discouraged. The damage to the steelwork increases the further aft the diver swims. What is left of the stern part of the *Sankisan Maru* also lies in very deep water, and this combination of damage and depth explains why few divers venture beyond the superstructure. The ship's stern section, including the rudder and propeller, lie separately from the rest of the vessel. The angle of the ship and the seabed around the stern are evidence that the *Sankisan* is lying in a crater made by the explosion that sank the ship.

Opposite: diver over the wreck of the Sankisan Maru.

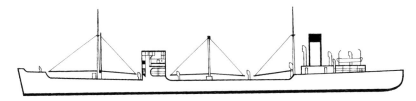

NAME:	SEIKO MARU.
TONNAGE:	5,386.
DIMENSIONS:	120.4m x 16.1m x 9.1m
SHIP TYPE:	Freighter (five holds).
SUNKEN ATTITUDE:	Upright with slight list to starboard.
DEPTH TO SEABED:	52m.
DEPTH TO WRECK:	29m (to bridge).
FEATURES OF NOTE:	Bow gun.

BUILT by Harima Dockyard near Osaka in 1940, the *Seiko Maru* was one of the Darien Kisen line of ships. It was not long before she was taken over by the Japanese military forces for use in the war. It would have been after this requisition that the bow gun was fitted. Even at the time of this refit, the gun would have been considered an old one.

The *Seiko Maru* received a single bomb hit near the port quarter, and judging from the damage in this aft area, would have sunk very rapidly stern first. The configuration of the *Seiko Maru* is unusual in that she has a midships superstructure and a stern superstructure very like a tanker. No wonder the US pilots who attacked the vessel originally mistook it for an "oiler" or tanker.

DIVING INFORMATION
THE raked bow area is protected by deck rails, and supports a very elderly piece of artillery. This gun was originally mounted on two wooden-spoked wheels, and only one remains. The gun now plays host to many different colourful corals and sponges, so any examination of its workings is difficult. As well as the bow gun, the visiting diver will also notice the anchor winch and chains leading forward to the anchor hawse pipes.

Number 1 and 2 holds are separated by the foremast, cargo derricks, and two ventilators. This mast reaches up to within 7.5m of the surface, and with its anemones and corals offers a satisfactory wreck feature with which to end the dive. Hatch cover beams for the first hold remain intact. The midships superstructure rises two decks above main deck level, and although the wooden decking has since rotted away, the ship's telegraph and the rest of the bridge is still worth a few photographs. The deck cabins aft of the bridge were evidently the crews' quarters, as several artefacts found in this area attest.

Aft of the midships superstructure, the diver will find Numbers 3 and 4 holds separated by a substantial kingpost to which the cargo derricks have been lashed. Number 5 hold is raised one deck above the main deck, and it is here, on the port side, that the diver will find a gaping hole in the ship's hull. This is big enough to swim through. The jagged-edged hole was created by the bomb hit, and the resulting explosion, so close to the ship's engine room, ignited the ship's fuel. The resulting fire burned with such an intensity that it added to the damage of the explosion by buckling stanchions and melting rails.

The aft superstructure is raised one deck above the last hold, and contains more cabins, as well as the ship's engine room. There are gangways down both port and starboard sides of this superstructure, and above these can be found the boat deck and lifeboat davits. Also on the boat deck, the diver will find the impressive funnel, the remains of three pairs of ventilators, and the engine-room skylights.

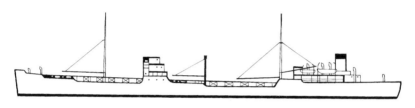

NAME:	SHINKOKU MARU.
TONNAGE:	10,020.
DIMENSIONS:	152.4m x 19.8m x 11.2m.
SHIP TYPE:	Tanker.
SUNKEN ATTITUDE:	Upright on even keel.
DEPTH TO SEABED:	39m.
DEPTH TO WRECK:	13m (to bridge) 18m (to deck).
FEATURES OF NOTE:	Bridge area, galley, surgeon's quarters,
	bow gun, human remains, marine life.

BUILT in 1939 by the Kawasaki Jyuko Company of Kobe, the *Shinkoku Maru* was powered by a single 8-cylinder diesel engine that generated some 3927hp. This huge ship was used to transport its capacity of 93,000 barrels of crude oil from America to Japan.

Requisitioned as a Fleet Tanker by the Imperial Japanese Navy in August, 1941, the *Shinkoku Maru* was fitted with two deck guns. Other additions included various structural reinforcements as well as a tripod mast on the aft superstructure. This was fitted to carry the long, heavy, fuel lines during the mid-sea refuelling of warships. On December 3 that year, the *Shinkoku Maru,* along with seven other tankers, refuelled the Japanese battle fleet sailing to attack Pearl Harbour in Hawaii.

In May-June 1942 the *Shinkoku Maru* and four other tankers refuelled the main Japanese battle group sailing to attack Midway island. Then on August 17, that year, while about 35 nautical miles west of Truk, the *Shinkoku Maru* was torpedoed by a submarine. This single strike proved insufficient to sink the 10,020-ton tanker, and the *Shinkoku Maru* escaped to Truk Lagoon, where the necessary repairs were made. Two months later, when the ship was seaworthy again, it resumed its task of supplying Truk and other islands with fuel oil from Japan. Military records next mention the ship having been attacked by yet another submarine on July 7, 1943. The damage was relatively minor, because the ship reported that although its forward Number 2 tank (containing 1,400 tons of light oil) was holed and flooded, it was able to make port for repairs. This time the repairs were made in Singapore, a port that had fallen to the Japanese during February, 1942. The repaired *Shinkoku Maru* left Singapore on August 15, 1943, only five weeks after the attack.

The *Shinkoku Maru* reportedly arrived at Truk Lagoon on February 14, 1944. Operation Hailstone began three days later, and the *Shinkoku Maru* could well have been one of the tankers spotted by US pilots north-west of Moen in the early part of the first day. By about midday it was attacked while at anchor north of Param island. Douglas Dauntless bombers from the US carrier *Yorktown* reported a direct hit amidships with one of their bombs.

Still afloat on February 18, the *Shinkoku Maru* was again attacked in a reported position east of Eot. It was just after 07.00 when the Grumman Avengers of the US carrier *Bunker Hill* jettisoned six torpedoes to sink the tanker. In the confusion of war the complete story of this vessel's sinking was lost. It is a matter of record, however, that the first attacking Avenger was credited with the only torpedo hit of this attack. The ordnance struck the *Shinkoku Maru* on the port side, towards the stern. This caused a serious fire, killing many members of the crew. The ship rapidly filled with water and sank stern first.

The *Shinkoku Maru* sank in a position 2 nautical miles north of Param, and about 4 nautical miles west-south-west of Moen. It now lies upright in 40m of water, with the pungent, heavy fumes of fuel oil permanently in evidence on the surface above the wreck. The deck can be easily reached at a depth of 18m.

DIVING INFORMATION

THE bow of this very long ship is slightly raked, and both anchor chains lead out of their respective hawse-pipes and down to the seabed at 36.5m. Sharks can quite frequently be observed at varying depths around this portion of the wreck. Moving aft, the diver will notice little coral growth on the foredeck. The deck rails are also noticeably absent. The two heavy-duty anchor winches are located just forward of the raised gun platform and forward deck gun. This weapon appears to have a calibre of 3in, and is cloaked in various corals. It lies at a depth of 12m, and the ambient light level is usually high enough for some good photographs, particularly around midday. An armoured shield protects the artillery piece from nothing now, as coral has invaded everywhere. There are four crates of ammunition on the plat-

Opposite: medicine bottles on operating table, Shinkoku Maru.

form behind this forward-facing barrel, and one of these crates is open. Inside, the diver will see 16 rounds of ready ammunition, but as the explosive charge for these is as unstable as the other ammunition in the lagoon, divers are advised to look but not touch.

The forecastle below the bow gun may be entered by either the port or starboard doorways. There is enough light for a casual look inside, but even at this shallow depth a torch is a necessity if penetrative exploration is planned. The first sights to greet the diver here are cables, hose coils, ropes, and other lines. The bosun's locker once held a number of running lights for the Shinkoku Maru, but many of these have been removed to the Truk museum. It is possible to find other lanterns inside, as well as an assortment of paint tins. Divers should be aware of the thick layer of silt throughout all the cabins on this ship, so finning should be kept to a minimum while inside it. Divers should also bear in mind that if they try to fin too far above the silt, they risk snagging their pillar valves or hoses on the web of electrical cabling that hangs in great tangled loops from the ceiling or deckhead. Such cabling now sags from its original position because the thin cable ties have rotted.

The foreship stretches for about 35m until the midship superstructure is reached. This foreship contains storage areas for dozens of 6m lengths of transfer hose, as well as the huge tanks/holds used for holding the fuel oil cargo of the Shinkoku Maru. The two huge oil tanks aft of the forecastle are surmounted by a long length of metal piping, with assorted valves and gauges. This pipe bridge extends along the length of the ship, over all of the storage tanks. It was, of course, used for loading and unloading the thousands of tons of oil cargo.

The midships superstructure alone is worth more than one dive. The three levels of cabins rise from the main deck, which lies at a depth of 20m, to the roof of the bridge at a depth of only 13m. Starting at the flying bridge at the top of this superstructure, there is a single engine telegraph for transmitting engine instructions to the engineer below decks at the aft end of the *Shinkoku Maru*. The wooden decking here has all but vanished, leaving only a metal gridwork of support beams. Swimming down through these, the diver gets onto the bridge itself. Here he will see the ship's helm, flanked by two engine telegraphs. The wooden wheel has since rotted away from the helm, and the direction indicator, as well as the voice tube on the side, are almost completely covered in coral. Secured to various bulkheads here, the diver will see a number of speech tubes descending through the deck to the lower levels. Also in evidence is the ship's compass, secured to the front bulkhead of the bridge at window level. Other finds include some lanterns with blue glass, and a large clock. The corals at this shallow depth are extremely prolific and colourful. Sponges, clams, algae, and gorgonias thrive over most artefacts of the *Shinkoku Maru*, making it a photographer's delight. One coral-free object, though, is a large brass gilt chest. This was found to contain small glass jars of pills, as well as sheaves of writing paper and pens. Although fragmented and extremely fragile, the Japanese kanji writing is clearly legible. This and a telephone have obviously been brought up to the shallower depths to allow more time for investigation.

Descending one deck from the bridge, the diver will find himself in either the galley or the officers' quarters. The galley contains a stove in good condition. Heaped on top of it are stacks of plates, dishes, cups, a teapot, and various bottles. These would have been stored in cupboards and cabinets that have obviously rotted away. Divers have collected the crockery and placed it all in one place for future visitors to enjoy. Lying on the floor there is also a large metal hot water container or boiler. Swimming aft through doorways the diver will find the cabins getting more spacious, but the large spaces give a false impression of life aboard the vessel, for much of this deck was partitioned off with plywood which has since disappeared. This is a good deck on which to find personal artefacts, and finds here include a generator, a bathroom and toilet, decorative glass lamps, officers' uniforms, a large chest of Japanese aluminium "Sen" coins, sake cups, bottles, and a typewriter. Towards the aft end of this deck level, in what used to be the officers' wardroom, is a large chest or box containing a magnificent array of glass wine decanters, glasses, cut-glass vases, sake bowls, plates, dishes, assorted boxes, and other discoveries. The best way to find this is by entering one of the doors in the aft bulkhead, rather than picking your way through the web of dangling electric cables on this deck.

Descending one deck further still, and entering the midships superstructure from the lower level on port side, the diver will find the ship's sick bay and operating theatre. This is a very interesting and major feature of the *Shinkoku Maru*, and one that should not be missed, if only because it is all but unique in Truk Lagoon. The silt in here is very thick in places, and photographers would do well to get here before other divers, and plan their photographs before they enter. The reason is simple: silt starts raining down from the ceiling or deck head and rising from the floor as soon as divers enter this large deck area. This problem is compounded by the darkness in this room thanks to the portholes being completely overgrown by sponges and soft corals. Along the port side of this cabin, only about 8-10m inside the doorway, is an operating table, with various medicine bottles, pill jars, and other multi-coloured containers lying around it or standing on the operating table itself. Drawers in this room hold even more medicine jars, as well as syringes. Behind this table is a fairly large, metal, circular container with smoke-blackened gauges on its side. This was apparently the surgeon's sterilisation unit. Next to this the diver will see a sink, presumably used for scrubbing out, and the blankets used by patients can be found hanging over a beam on the cabin wall. These must have once been stored on wooden shelves that have all since been eaten away by wood-boring organisms. As well as all the medical artefacts, there is a pile of old gramophone records, and a light fitting which hangs motionless from the ceiling. Other features on this deck level include a bathtub, urinals and a Japanese toilet. You can easily leave the operating theatre and sick bay by finning aft and out of another doorway on the port side, thus avoiding the clouds of silt that inevitably rise behind you as you enter.

The aftship superstructure and crews' quarters are the larger of the two supered by about 50m of cargo tanks, and this distance should not be underestimated. It is a long swim. Moving aft from the midships superstructure, the diver will notice an abundance of circular and oval shaped hard corals lying almost casually on the deck. Swimming aft from the midships superstructure, once you have reached the kingpost mast, you are one-third of the way to the aft superstructure. The pipe bridge continues in a straight line over the top of the cargo tanks all the way to the stern. As with its forward counterpart, there are valves and flanges to facilitate the loading and discharge of the oil cargo. This piping does not lie over the central line of the ship, but is set to one side. The stern section of the ship lies in slightly deeper water than the bows. This is a much bigger area of cabins than its forward counterpart, and a lot darker in places too.

Starting with the upper portions of this section, the diver cannot fail to notice the huge single funnel towering towards the surface. This and much of the upper boat deck are covered in a colourful living tapestry of corals. The marine life here is some of the best you can see in the lagoon, and definitely worth a roll or two of film. The engine room skylights are located just forward of the huge funnel, and are open, allowing easy access or egress to this part of the ship. The portholes set in these skylights remain intact, even after the explosion that took place beneath them. Apart from the funnel, there are the remains of lifeboat davits, and ventilator shafts which go below decks. Just behind the funnel there is the huge tripod mast fitted for the ship's military role, and used for carrying the fuel lines during ship-to-ship refuelling. (The control room for this transfer of fuel oil can be found one deck lower, nearby, but is very cramped and restricting. It is full of assorted

Left: ladder on a coral-covered deck of the Shinkoku Maru.

deck lower, nearby, but is very cramped and restricting. It is full of assorted gauges, valves, and dials). Also in this area a samurai sword, complete with scabbard, has been found. This has since been hidden, and its location is known only to a few dive guides who may show it to their customers. Continuing aft, the diver will see a pair of ventilator shafts, then the uppermost deck drops one level to where the stern gun is mounted on a raised gun platform. This, as with so much on the upper decks, is festooned with sponges, algae, soft and hard corals.

The aftship superstucture can easily be entered by either the port or starboard doors at main deck level. Each opens onto a passageway that leads into the stern of the ship on either side of the engine room tower. Cabins are located off each corridor. Entry into these cabin areas is easy, but divers should be cautioned about the drooping cables that have sagged, and in some places dropped altogether, from the deck head or ceiling. As well as this hazard, the silt and muck that has settled in the current-free cabins is in some places quite substantial. Be careful that this does not rise up behind you and obscure your exit.

Outside the starboard doorway is a collection of artefacts, presumably brought out from the cabins inside. These include a ceramic water filter, with the inscription completely in English, a wellington boot, the remains of a deck head lamp, a fire extinguisher and other items. Entering this starboard passageway the diver will find the crews' mess on the right, and another cabin which may have been the engineer's, on the left. Both of these cabins contain bones which are quite obviously human. Divers are requested to show these dead men the respect they deserve. Look but do not touch. A larger cabin may be found further along the passageway on the left, and judging from the number of blankets in here this could well have been the crews' quarters. Other finds in these cabins include sinks, taps, coils of electrical wire, a briefcase, sake bottles, and assorted crockery. More cabins and further passageways are found deeper into the ship, but because of the extreme problem with silt, these should only be explored by divers proficient in the use of a rope or line. It should also be noted that not all skulls have been bleached clean by the sea. Divers should therefore examine every object thoroughly before picking it up.

The port doorway into the aftship superstructure is opposite its starboard equivalent. There is a cabin on the left which may well have been someone's quarters, and another much larger room behind it which is almost certainly crews' accommodation – there are remains of two-tier bunks in here, as well as some human remains, broken glass and a couple of beer bottles. The port passageway continues aft like its starboard counterpart, but this time the diver has light shining in from ahead. The next door on the left behind the crews' quarters gives access into the engine room tower.

A catwalk and steps lead down to the engine cylinder heads, and a depth of 33m. Each of the eight cylinder heads is secured by a dozen huge bolts to its respective cylinder. The wires that you will see coming out of the cylinders was supposedly connected to monitoring equipment, so the engineer could check the engine's performance. Light bulbs and their circular light shades hang remarkably hole in the hull can clearly be seen on the port side. Various water, steam and fuel pipes are plumbed along the bulkheads, with assorted gauges and dials also in evidence. There is a water separator, a fuel injection pump, and even an auxiliary engine. Evidently there was time enough for a fire before water pouring in from the torpedo hole sank the *Shinkoku Maru*. This is clear from the smoke-blackened glass of the gauges here. The glass of these gauges, though, is not cracked or melted as it would be in a serious, longburning fire, so that means the engine room was completely flooded after about 20 or 30 minutes. Exit from the engine room can be made either from the skylights directly above, at a depth of around 18m, from the torpedo hole in the port side, or doorways into the starboard or port passageways mentioned earlier. Aft of the engine room, the diver will find another mess room with a CO_2 fire extinguisher, and some crockery. Another cabin contains an electric motor, a drum of electric cable, and other lines. There are also reports of a spare propeller blade bolted to a bulkhead further aft. Apparently this blade is of a different design from that fitted to the *Shinkoku Maru*, and could not therefore have been fitted on this ship.

Near the engine room doorway in the port passageway it is possible to ascend a set of stairs one deck further. The cabins here are positioned above the port passageway. Plenty of light comes into these cabins from open doorways and portholes, so the diver can continue out into the open sea, or remain and explore the officers' quarters on this boat deck. Finds here include a toilet, sink and urinal, as well as a ceramic-tiled Japanese-style bathroom. This has two smaller tubs next to a much larger square tub. Each of these tubs was served by a set of taps that remain in excellent condition.

The ship's propeller and rudder can be seen at a depth of 39m, and around here too, on the port side, the diver can see and swim into the torpedo hole that sank the *Shinkoku Maru*.

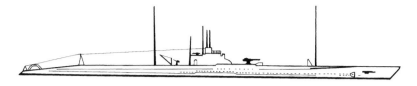

NAME:	SHINOHARA.(Submarine I-169).
TONNAGE:	1,400 (1,785 max, 2,440 submerged).
DIMENSIONS:	102.6m x 8.2m x 4.5m.
SHIP TYPE:	I-168 class (Type Kaidai 6A) submarine.
SUNKEN ATTITUDE:	30 degree list to port.
DEPTH TO SEABED:	38m.
DEPTH TO WRECK:	34m (to deck).
FEATURES OF NOTE:	Basically intact except for depth charge damage to conning tower and foreship.

BUILT by Mitsubishi works of Kobe, just west of Osaka, the *I-69* was launched on February 15, 1934, and was then renumbered the *I-169* in May, 1942. It was a large submarine for the time, and was one of the KD 6A (I-168) class. Driven by its twin propellers at a speed of 10 knots, the vessel had a range of 14,000 miles. When submerged and travelling at 3 knots, the vessel could travel 65 miles before having to surface. The *I-69* was armed with six 21in torpedo tubes, a 3.9in deck gun, and a 13mm AA gun. It was capable of descending to 75m, and had a complement of 70 men.

The submarine's first recorded action was while it was attached to the 6th Submarine Fleet (based at Kwajalein). The *I-69* was just one of 30 Japanese submarines taking part in the attack of Pearl Harbour, on December 7, 1941. While patrolling off the south coast of Oahu island, the *I-69* got fouled in some anti-submarine netting.

The captain ordered various forward and backward manouvres, coupled with the blowing and re-filling of ballast tanks, all to no avail. The crew then settled down for a last meal as the air ran out. When they had finished, it was decided to make one last desperate attempt to release the craft, and using full speed astern, this succeeded. Fortunately for the submarine and its crew, there was no US shipping in the area, and the *I-69* was able to replenish its air tanks.

The *I-169* went on to serve in the Japanese offensive at Midway during late May and early June of 1942. The following year, the submarine was converted to carry cargo, and steamed to the Aleutians in the far north of the Pacific. Here, after 15 trips to and from Japan, the *I-169* and seven other subs, dropped off 120 tons of stores, and collected 820 men from the beleaguered garrison. During November that same year, the *I-169* and eight other submarines were ordered on to the Gilbert islands to assist against the allied invasion there. With the Allied grip on the Pacific theatre tightening, the Kwajalein home base of the 6th Submarine

Fleet, was becoming untenable. The Japanese therefore decided in January of 1944 to move the 6th Submarine Fleet to Truk Lagoon.

The *I-169*, or *Shinohara*, named after its captain, Lt. Commander Shigeo Shinohara, returned to Truk from patrol on April 1, 1944. While loading stores and provisions for its next voyage, the *Shinohara* was forced to dive to the bottom during an air raid on April 2. The submarine never re-surfaced, and still lies where it sought refuge from that air raid. Apparently the upper valve of the storm ventilation tube, located in the conning tower, had not been closed properly. It is also believed that in their rush to take evasive action, another valve at one of the torpedo loading hatches was also not closed properly. This consequently flooded the main control room, and the forward compartment. With the ballast tank controls inaccessible, the crew were prevented from taking any effective measures to surface. When the air raid was over, and all submarines except the *Shinohara* had resurfaced, a diver was sent down in standard hard hat dress. He reported that although the control room was flooded, he had tapped on all of the remaining five hatches and received hammered responses from the sailors trapped inside. The crew had obviously managed to secure the watertight doors on either side of the control room, but were now sitting in what was to become their coffin and tomb. The air raids continued, and despite rescue attempts, using a 30-ton salvage crane, and many dives to secure cables around the submarine's hull none of the crew could be saved. The amount of water inside the vessel had increased its weight to an impossible degree for lifting purposes. By 23.30 on April 3, 1944, all internal tapping noises had ceased.

Over the next six weeks the Japanese recovered from 13 to 35 bodies. This was by no means all there were, but with the likelihood of a US invasion increasing, the military authorities decided to depth charge the areas that were now cleared of crew. With the conning tower and control room thus destroyed, any effective US salvage of the submarine was prevented.

Following Al Giddings' discovery of the wreck in 1971, the Japanese government started a project to raise the remaining dead of the *Shinohara*. A joint Japanese-American expedition was then given a budget of 3 million Yen to perform the task. In Al Giddings' film, he claims the expedition recovered 84 crew members. Subsequent books describe 35 intact, and 35-40 broken skulls. What is not contested is the fact that there were more than the sub's complement of 70 killed in this tragedy. It is therefore assumed that either workers involved in the loading of stores, or a contingent of Japanese marines were on board.

All of the crew raised were subsequently given the Shinto burial rites appropriate to their religion.

The *Shinohara* still claims life. A diver became trapped under the gratings of the engine room and drowned within sight of his exit in April, 1974. All visitors should therefore afford this particular wreck the maximum amount of respect. Before any diver considers entering the *Shinohara*, it should be borne in mind that the cramped conditions of a submarine are far more dangerous than the cabins and cargo holds of any ship.

DIVING INFORMATION

THE bow and foreship are extensively damaged. The torpedo tubes are recognisable in the heap of twisted hull plating, and smaller finds such as sailors' boots can still be made. Swimming aft, the diver will notice the submarine's deck gun in the wreckage at a depth of 40m. This was a 3.9in gun, that had been fixed just forward of the conning tower. Further aft still and the wreckage of the conning tower becomes unrecognisable as such. For the most part, the midships and forward section of the *Shinohara* are not as intact as the section aft of where the conning tower used to be.

The stern half of the submarine is in better condition than the forward area. The wooden deck boards have all since disappeared, but the steel supports remain, along with the three deck hatches into the submarine itself. The 13mm AA gun was positioned aft of the conning tower, but there is no sign of this now. The pressure hull here at the stern is intact, and divers can see that the submarine lists about 30 degrees to port. Almost no coral grows on the vessel, so few of the *Shinohara*'s features are obscured.

Moving towards the stern, the diver will see many air hoses, and steel lifting cables still wrapped around the hull. These were used in the desperate but vain attempts to save the crews' lives. Continuing aft, it is impossible to miss the starboard muffler, while its port counterpart remains buried in the seabed and decking. The last deck hatch leads to the engine room, and it was this hatch that Al Giddings' expedition used to gain access into the submarine. About a metre aft of this hatch there is the stout tripod mast used as both antenna and flag pole. Moving further aft, the decking drops considerably to the stern. This again was sabotaged by the Japanese, to prevent any US attempts at salvage. Down at a depth of 42m only the starboard propeller remains on its shaft, but this is damaged. The port screw is missing. Above the prop shafts divers will see two exhaust ports with their pipes curving outward and then back in to the engine room itself.

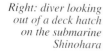

Right: diver looking out of a deck hatch on the submarine Shinohara

Overleaf: gauges in the engine room of the Susuki Maru

NAME:	SUB-CHASER.
TONNAGE:	300 (approx).
DIMENSIONS:	25.9m x 5.5m x 1.9m.
SHIP TYPE:	Naval anti-submarine vessels.
SUNKEN ATTITUDE:	Capsized.
DEPTH TO SEABED:	16m.
DEPTH TO WRECK:	3m (keel).
FEATURES OF NOTE:	Sonar type device on hull.

THERE is an element of confusion over the identity of a wrecksite in shallow water on the west coast of Dublon Island. Its configuration and certain artefacts found on it seem to suggest it was once some sort of submarine chaser.

DIVING INFORMATION
THE fact that this wreck has capsized, and now lies upside down with much coral growth in 15m does not make identification easy. It lies 800m west of Dublon Island.

The first feature to be noted is the upturned hull and bilge keel. Mounted on the bilge keel is some form of round object that is securely fixed in a position away from the ship's hull. This is about 30cm in diameter, and about 25cm deep. It is attached to a heavy-duty extendable shaft that is also around 25cm across. It appears to be some form of sonar, which would of course be a feature expected on a sub-chaser of the time.

The wreck can be easily entered by swimming between the seabed and the deck, but the hull restricts a great deal of natural light, so any penetration of the wreck requires a reliable underwater torch. Divers should also be aware of the fact that a quantity of dirty engine oil has floated up inside the wreck and now lies trapped under various ledges as well as the hull itself.

The stern of the wreck is worth a visit to see how the propeller blades have bent over at the tips. This presumably was because the crew were attempting to run their vessel aground rather than lose her in deep water. The rudder appears to have been sheared off by this same manoeuvre, for there is no sign of it.

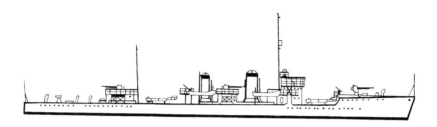

NAME:	The SUSUKI (Patrol Boat 34).
TONNAGE:	935 tons (displacement).
DIMENSIONS:	85.3m x 7.9m x 2.4m.
SHIP TYPE:	MOMI Class destroyer.
SUNKEN ATTITUDE:	Upright on sloping seabed.
DEPTH TO SEABED:	18m (at stern).
DEPTH TO WRECK:	3m (at bow deck) 11m (at stern).
FEATURES OF NOTE:	Assorted cupboards, boxes, gasmasks etc below deck.

BUILT in 1921 by Ishikawajima Zosensho of Tokyo, the *Susuki,* or *Sutsuki,* was a Momi-class destroyer. It had twin screws driven by two turbines that generated 12,000 shaft hp. This gave the vessel a maximum reported speed of 36 knots. Some of the fastest destroyers of their time, the 21 Momi-class craft were armed with two 21in torpedo tubes, three 4.7in guns, two 7.7mm AA guns, and four depth charge throwers and racks for 36 depth charges.

Nine of the Momi-class destroyers, including the *Susuki,* were refitted, reclassified, and renamed in 1939. Because of a design fault in the manufacture, these craft were top heavy. It was therefore deemed necessary to increase the ballast and raise the ship's displacement from 770 to 935 tons. By removing both of the torpedo tubes, one of the 4.7in guns, and half of the depth charges, these vessels were also made less top heavy. Other alterations included the removal of one of the boilers, and increasing facilities so that these modernised vessels could accommodate troops as well as the 110 crew members. Now capable of only 18 knots instead of 36, the *Susuki,* or *Patrol Boat 34* as it was renamed, was still a faster troop transport than the larger and more vulnerable cargo ships, because the destroyer's stern had been modified to carry and launch a Daihatsu landing craft capable of getting troops onto beaches or shallow coral reefs.

During June 1942, that *Patrol Boat 34* formed part of the Transport Group of the Midway Occupation force, and continued working until severely damaged by a collision with the Japanese destroyer *Yakaze* during March 1943. Satisfactory repairs could only be made at the fleet repair anchorage in Truk. *Patrol Boat 34* was therefore towed to the floating dry dock there, where its guns were removed, and a substitute bow fitted. The work was a hurried wartime improvisation, as divers will see for themselves.

Once the bow work was completed, the ship was tied to a buoy, and preparations apparently made for re-installing the deck guns and fitting anchors. Unfortunately the work of the marine engineers was all to no avail, for Truk was then bombed by US planes. There is an element of doubt, but *Patrol Boat 34* is believed to have been sunk during the raid on July 3, 1944.

DIVING INFORMATION

THE bow is an interesting feature of this wreck because of the ship's history. Clearly the crude lines of this makeshift metalwork betray the speed with which the new bow was made and fitted. The work to the bow was obviously unfinished because of the clear lack of any anchor. Because the depth to the bow deck is only 3-4m, this and most of the foreship are popular as a snorkelling site. *Patrol Boat 34* lies on sloping ground, pointing west, with a 20 degree list to port. There is not as much coral growing on this wreck as one might expect in the shallow water. Entry into the ship is easy, and several rotted holes in the hull make light penetration very good. There are some such holes in the port bow. There are few guard rails in evidence, but the metal decking remains remarkably intact, with only hatches offering access below decks. The deck gun here was removed from the bow before the repair work, however the gun platform remains. Finds in this area include a lantern, remains of a torpedo, bits of a torpedo firing tube, and even the tail section of one of the bombs that may have sank the ship.

Moving aft along this narrow-beamed vessel, the diver will come across little of the superstructure, as most of this seems to have been blown off. There are a couple of deck cabins to explore around the 5-6m mark, with the usual ventilator shafts looking like huge pillars because their cowls or scoops were blasted off. The *Susuki* had two small funnels but little remains of these, except for short stumps.

The engine room can be entered from the skylights or by a deck hatch further aft. Entering this particular engine room is much more of a serious undertaking than entering the larger cargo ships of the lagoon. Here the engine room is very cramped, and the diver should even consider removing his or her fins if entry is contemplated. Because of the rusty silt dislodged from the low ceiling or deck head by exhaled air bubbles, and the heavy layer of silt over the rest of the engine room, a line is definitely recommended for any search of this area. Once inside, the diver will notice the last of the two ship's boilers (the other having been removed during the 1939 alterations). There are also a variety of gauges, piping, and a large generator.

Aft of the engine room, the visitor will see two empty gun platforms and remains of the deck ventilators. It is possible to swim below decks here into several large roomy cabins. These have cupboards and lockers, crockery, lanterns and large food tins. Other reported finds here include an Arisaka infantry rifle, gas masks, uniforms, and medicine bottles. The high light level is due not only to the shallow water, but also the few holes that have rotted in the hull.

The stern deck lies at 9m, with the seabed here going down to 18m. Beware of the large drum-like objects on the deck here. They are depth charges, and definitely not to be knocked about! The decking at the stern is sloped slightly to carry the 150 man Daihatsu landing craft that would have been launched from here. It is unlikely such a craft would have been carried after the bows were damaged, so it is equally unlikely that such a landing craft will be found by divers around the wreck. Settling into the silt is an impressive pair of propellers, as well as the large square-shaped rudder.

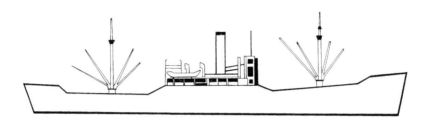

NAME:	TAIHO MARU.
TONNAGE:	2829 tons.
DIMENSIONS:	93m x 13.7m x 7m
SHIP TYPE:	Freighter.
SUNKEN ATTITUDE:	Lying on port beam.
DEPTH TO SEABED:	44m.
DEPTH TO WRECK:	27m.
FEATURES OF NOTE:	Two landing craft lying nearby. Stern gun on platform. Cargo of fuel oil drums.

BUILT by Hitachi Jyuko K.K. in 1943, this freighter was driven by a single reciprocal steam engine, which gave the vessel a maximum speed of 13.7 knots. At a time when Japan had already suffered defeats such as the Battle of Midway, the Battle of the Coral Sea, and Guadalcanal it was inevitable that shipping of this time be requisitioned for military use. The *Taiho Maru* was taken over from her owners, the Osaka Shosen Kaisha line, and used by the Japanese Navy from October 15, 1943.

The *Taiho Maru* received hits on the foreship and amidships from one of the first waves of February 17, 1944. The bow and foreship were then observed to disintegrate in an explosion at 12.05 that same day. The ship sank south of Fefan island, and about 1km to the west of Uman. It was found by Sam Redford in 1972, and has been lost and found several times since then. The *Taiho Maru* now lies on its port beam, with only the aft ship recognisable. Because the ship is not whole and intact, the *Taiho Maru* is very rarely dived.

DIVING INFORMATION

THE wreck lies in an underwater valley, with much of the seabed having been gouged out during the huge explosion that sank the ship. The bow, foreship, and midships area were destroyed in the explosion, and nothing has so far been found of this part of the vessel. The forward part of the wreck is a complete mess of twisted and buckled steelwork. Only by swimming aft will the diver be able to make any sense of what remains of the vessel.

Two landing craft had been tied up to the *Taiho Maru* at the time of the sinking, and these were dragged down with the vessel. They now lie on the seabed, at the forward part of what is left of the ship. Originally about 16m long, these boats would have been used to load and offload cargo as the islands of Truk did not have piers or jetties for the ships to tie up to. The boats have flat decks and a tiny bridge area, which still has intact portholes. Both landing craft lean up against the hull.

Number 3 hold contains many large fuel oil drums. It is highly likely that this cargo was being unloaded into the landing craft just before the explosion, for by comparison with the last hold, Number 3 hold is only half full. Moving aft of this hold, the diver will notice the aft mast, which remains remarkably intact. With the heavy list of the ship, it is no surprise that the cargo derricks all now point over to port.

Number 4 hold was filled with the same large fuel oil drums, and a great many of these have fallen out onto the seabed, making a big pile. Aft of this last hold, divers will find the poop deck, on which is mounted a circular gun platform and what appears to be a 3in howitzer. Moving around the stern, divers will also notice that it is squared off instead of the traditional rounded shape. Certain letters such as the 'A' and the 'I' of *Taiho Maru*, are visible on the stern. The rudder seems to have given in to gravity and now points to port, like everything else. The single propeller is of a four-bladed construction.

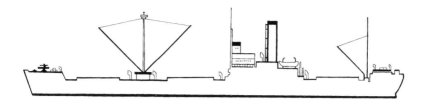

NAME:	TAIKICHI MARU.
TONNAGE:	1,891.
DIMENSIONS:	76m-87m long approx.
SHIP TYPE:	Freighter.
SUNKEN ATTITUDE:	Broken up over large area.
DEPTH TO SEABED:	30m.
DEPTH TO WRECK:	27m.
FEATURES OF NOTE:	Smoke stack and deck ventilators.

A CAPTURED Japanese message on Saipan apparently listed a ship called *Daikichi Maru* as being sunk at Truk Lagoon. An official Japanese Navy document, though, lists the 1,891 ton *Taikichi Maru* as being sunk there. It is possible that these ships are one and the same.

The *Taikichi Maru* was an aft-engined vessel with lines and proportions that would not have been too dissimilar from those of, say, the *Gosei Maru*. It remains for divers to find positive identification of the wreck that lies about 650m north of Fefan island, but circumstantial evidence seems to suggest that this is the *Taikichi Maru*. This wreck, however, is not dived very often at all.

The official attack reports of Operation Hailstone at the Naval Operational Archives Washington DC state that a tanker of an estimated size of between 4,000 and 5,500 tons was attacked by a plane from the US carrier *Bunker Hill* at around 00.25 during the first day. The pilot reports a hit with his 1,600lb bomb. In the afternoon of the same day, eight pilots from the same carrier conducted an attack that scored one decisive hit. The ordnance hit the ship amidships, and according to some of the pilots who witnessed it, the resulting explosion was a violent one. The location of this attack, the understandable confusion between an aft-engined tanker and an aft-engined cargo vessel, as well as the frequently overestimated tonnage of the ships these young pilots attacked, leads one to the assumption that this wreck was in fact the *Taikichi Maru*.

DIVING INFORMATION

THE 15m long bow section is one of the three distinctly separate chunks of this wreck. This piece contains the forecastle, but all decking and hull plating is severely torn and twisted. It lies in 30m, and also happens to be about 30m away from the larger stern section.

The stern section is the largest chunk of surviving wreckage, and contains the

aft engine room, as well as the smoke stack, which remarkably survived the vast blast which obviously ripped the ship apart. Lifeboat davits and ventilators can also be made out. This part of the ship has all but fallen right over onto its side, but orientation problems stem more from the results of a huge bomb explosion rather than vertical decks.

A much smaller, third section of wreckage lies nearby, and seems to carry the remains of one of the masts and something of a deck cabin.

Because few people have ventured onto this wreck site it remains something of an unsolved mystery.

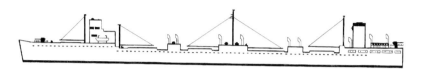

NAME:	TONAN MARU No 3.
TONNAGE:	19,209 tons.
DIMENSIONS:	163.m x 22.5m x 17.3m.
SHIP TYPE:	Whale factory converted into tanker.
SUNKEN ATTITUDE:	Only remnants remain following salvage.
DEPTH TO SEABED:	34m.
DEPTH TO WRECK:	32m.
FEATURES OF NOTE:	Parts of aft superstructure remain.

BUILT in 1938 by Osaka Tekkosho of Osaka, the *Tonan Maru No 3* was powered by two reciprocating steam engines that drove the ship's twin screws. This gave the whale factory ship a maximum reported speed of 14.1 knots. Though designed for long periods of duty in the Antarctic, converting whale blubber into oil, the *Tonan Maru No 3* was soon requisitioned and pressed into military service as a fleet oil tanker.

On July 24, 1943, west of Truk, the eastbound *Tonan Maru* was attacked by the American submarine USS *Tinosa*. Commander Dan Daspit had spotted the lone tanker, and quickly manoeuvred his submarine into the best attack position he could. From 4000yds astern of his prey the submarine commander fired a spread of four torpedoes. Two of these hit the target at an oblique angle and exploded, causing the *Tonan Maru* to stop dead in her tracks. The American submarine commander was then able to take his time in manoeuvring the *Tinosa* into a better firing position 875yds off the starboard beam. One of the two largest tankers the Japanese had, seemed doomed. Her crew could only open fire on either the submarine's periscope, or the torpedo wakes as they charged inexorably towards the 19,209 ton tanker, that was immobile and listing to port. From his near perfect

Opposite: live mines in a hold
of the San Francisco Maru.

position, and unthreatened by any form of Japanese escort, Commander Daspit spent the next few hours firing eleven torpedoes into the *Tonan Maru No 3*. One by one each of these travelled unerringly towards their target, only to bounce harmlessly off the ship's hull and sink. The Commander's frustration can only be imagined. He ordered examination after examination of each torpedo, and seemed to cover every eventuality except altering his position to a more oblique firing angle. The arrival of a Japanese destroyer forced Commander Daspit to retire from the engagement. *Tonan Maru No 3* was towed safely to Truk Lagoon, while the *Tinosa* took its last torpedo for tests at Pearl Harbour.

It was this incident that highlighted the unsuitability of the Mark 6 contact detonator in the Mark XIV torpedoes. Following extensive tests in Hawaii, it was found that only when the torpedo hit at an angle was there any chance of the charge being detonated.

For six and a half months, the Japanese marine engineers of Truk worked to repair the severe damage sustained by the *Tonan Maru No 3*. With such a high priority given to fleet oil tankers, though, it was inevitable that one of the first naval targets of Operation Hailstone would be the *Tonan Maru No 3*. So it was that on the first morning of these attacks, the tanker received two direct hits on the stern. Throughout February 17, 1944, the ship settled into the water. The following day brought further attacks, with at least one hit by a Douglas Dauntless dive bomber of the US carrier *Yorktown*.

The *Tonan Maru* represented a huge investment at the time, and even after the war the Japanese authorities considered its salvage an economically viable option. The tanker was therefore raised on March 3, 1951, and refitted in Japan. It was renamed simply the *Tonan Maru*, and served as a civilian factory ship until it was eventually scrapped in 1971.

DIVING INFORMATION

THOUGH the ship was raised in 1951, there remains a great deal of wreckage at the sight where the *Tonan Maru No 3* turned turtle and sank. Sections of decking and hull plating complete with portholes have been identified along with ventilator shafts, lifeboat davits, and what is believed to be the port funnel. All lie in various heaps at a depth of 34m. Particularly of interest to the diver are the concentric circles of the Nippon Suisan K.K. shipping line, on the outboard side of one of the ship's two funnels.

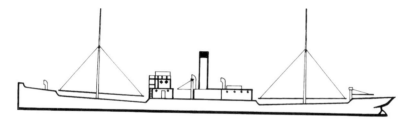

NAME: UNKAI MARU No 6.
TONNAGE: 3,220 tons.
DIMENSIONS: 100.8m x 14.9m x 6.6m.
SHIP TYPE: Freighter.
SUNKEN ATTITUDE: Upright on even keel.
DEPTH TO SEABED: 44m.
DEPTH TO WRECK: 23m to gun.
FEATURES OF NOTE: Bow and stern areas.

BUILT in 1905 by William Grey & Co. Ltd of West Hartlepool in England, this
five-hold freighter was powered by a single Blair & Co diesel engine. This reportedly gave the vessel a maximum speed of 12 knots. Initially named and launched
as the *Venus*, the *Unkai Maru* was bought by the Japanese in 1911 for £32,500.

At anchor north of Uman island, and south of Eten airfield, the *Unkai Maru No
6* was bombed throughout the first day of Operation Hailstone. The ship received
four reported bomb hits from aircraft, and was still afloat on the second day of the
attack. The attack reports indicate two further bomb hits, and three near misses
during February 18, 1944. The bows of the vessel were seen to lift out of the water
during this last attack, but the sinking of the *Unkai Maru No 6* was not observed.

The wreck was located by Klaus Lindemann in July 1980, and lies approximately 700m north of Uman island.

DIVING INFORMATION
THE bow of this ship is a plumb type, with no rake whatsoever. The depth here is
23m, and because of this shallow water, corals cover much of the 3in deck gun as
well as the gun platform on which it sits. The barrel points straight ahead, and as it
has no elevation, it is a fair assumption that it was not used against the attacking
aircraft of 1944. Ammo crates are located on the gun platform just behind the
breech, and these are just as covered in sessile marine life as the gun. The diver
will also see the two anchor chains leading from the winch out to each hawsepipe.
An open deck hatch can be seen near these large chains, and this hatch affords
access into the lower decks of the forecastle. The decking here has rotted in
places, so that a diver need not rely on hatches to get below decks. Access into
these forward cabins may also be made from either of two doors at main deck
level. The forward-most cabin beneath the forecastle deck, contains a treasure

trove of personal artefacts, and is well worth a visit. There are mugs, cutlery, gilt uniform buttons and a teapot, and reported finds include an inkpot, soldering lamp, and sake bottles. Another reason for venturing into the cabins of the forecastle is that having entered from the port doorway at main deck level, the diver is confronted with an array of several large bronze ship's lanterns. The bosun's locker in which they are stored is very confined, but these lanterns make fine subjects for photography.

Number 1 hold has many of its hatch cover beams in place, but it is still easy to enter and descend to a depth of 36m. This hold contains heaps of boxes and crates, as well as gas masks, assorted bottles and shoes. One interesting find in this hold, though, heaped against a bulkhead, is several stacks of china marked with the five pointed star of the Imperial Japanese Army. The two forward holds are separated by a tiny mast house and foremast of unusually square cross-section. The uppermost portion of this mast has fallen down, and has brought down many of the steel rigging lines with it. The derricks used for craning cargo in and out of these two forward holds are still mounted on this foremast.

Number 2 hold is largely empty of interesting cargo, and there have been no reports of interesting finds in here.

The midships superstructure and the smaller Number 3 hold were subjected not only to the bomb hits, but also an intensive and long-burning fire before the ship sank. Smoke from this fire reportedly rose 4-5000 feet in the air before the vessel sank. The devastation in the bridge and cabins should not therefore be a surprise to the visiting diver. Ascending two decks above main deck level, the diver will find the ship's bridge. The explosions on the port side, and intense fire here, have taken their toll not only on the contents of this part of the vessel, but also the metal structure of the decking and support beams. The ship's telegraph and rudderstand have fallen or been blown over, and now lie in the large amount of silt and muck that cover the bridge decking. Other finds to look out for here are the ship's large sponge- and algae-encrusted bell, as well as the ship's strongbox. Evidently much of the bridge was made of wood, and this of course was burned away in the two-day fire that raged on board.

Number 3 hold is a much smaller stowage area than the other four holds. This hold forms something of a shaft between the *Unkai Maru*'s bridge and the engine room. The cargo would have been hoisted in and out of this hold by the derricks mounted on the small kingpost mast which is positioned at the aft edge of the hold. If any cargo was being carried in this hold during the attack of 1944, then it was burned away in the fierce fire following the 500lb bomb hits. This hold appears empty of any interesting finds. Aft of the hold, the diver will find the boats deck, complete with lifeboat davits, two ventilators, the funnel and engine-room skylights. The ventilators and ship's funnel show no sign of pressure damage from explosions, and appear to have just fallen during or after the sinking. The two wide bands at the top of the funnel are the mark of the Japanese shipping company Nakamura Kisen K.K., who owned the *Unkai Maru*.

The engine room may be entered from the open skylights. These are between the lifeboat davits, aft of where the funnel originally came through the decking. Descending to a depth of 38m, this engine room can be seen to be severely damaged. This again was due to the onboard fire. Various pieces of machinery, and block and tackle can be made out, but little else of interest has remained. This part of the ship was gutted by fire.

Numbers 4 and 5 holds are separated by the aft mast, two cargo winches and a great deal of steel rigging lines. This aft mast, like its forward counterpart, is also square in cross section. Both of the aft holds are empty of cargo, but the diver will notice the large propeller shaft tunnel running along the bottom of each of these holds.

The sterncastle rises one deck above main deck level, but unlike the forecastle, it does not have a deck gun. This area is interesting to visit because of the antiquated steering assembly. Unlike the more modern ships of this era, the steering assembly of the *Unkai Maru* is not housed inside the sterncastle, but outside, exposed to the elements. This assembly is composed of the rudder drive, which is a double-winch type apparatus bolted to the deck. This is then linked by huge chains, each running around one of two circular sections, which in turn are securely fixed to the rudderpost.

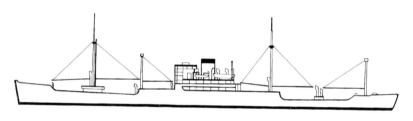

NAME:	YAMAGIRI MARU.
GROSS TONNAGE:	6,438.
DIMENSIONS:	134m x 17.7m x 9.7m.
SHIP TYPE:	Passenger-freighter.
SUNKEN ATTITUDE:	Lies on port side.
DEPTH TO SEABED:	34m.
DEPTH TO WRECK:	15m.
FEATURES OF NOTE:	Steam-roller in hold Number 5 and large 46cm shells for the battleships *Yamato* and *Musashi* in hold Number 6.

BUILT in 1939 by Mitsubishi Jukogyo of Yokohama, this large, six-hold freighter had a single screw, driven by a 4976hp diesel engine that gave the ship a maximum speed of 17 knots. As with most of the Japanese shipping of the time, the *Yamagiri Maru* was requisitioned by the military for the war effort from September 15, 1941.

The *Yamagiri Maru* was torpedoed by the American submarine USS *Drum* on August 28, 1943, while sailing in the Bismarck sea off Papua New Guinea. The ship made it back to Rabaul, New Britain, for repairs, but not long after this, Rabaul itself became the focus of Allied bombing raids in the Pacific theatre of war. The *Yamagiri* was apparently photographed in Rabaul about one month after the torpedo incident, but with all the nearby islands having fallen back into Allied hands, it was evidently not safe for the ship to remain there. It could also have been that more major repairs were required on the *Yamagiri Maru*. Whatever the reason, it sailed, or was towed, to the Combined Fleet repair anchorage east of Dublon island in Truk Lagoon.

For five and a half months, marine engineers had worked to repair the *Yamagiri Maru*. Then, on February 17, 1944, US pilots scored several bomb hits and near misses during the first day of Operation Hailstone. At around 08.20 the following day, the *Yamagiri Maru* was again attacked, and this time received hits by a 1,000lb bomb, and at least one 500lb bomb. The resulting explosions then started a fire that sent smoke thousands of feet into the air. The *Yamagiri* was not observed to sink by the attacking pilots, but the vessel now lies in a position near where it was photographed during this attack. That is approximately 750m north of Fefan, and 1.8km east of Dublon.

The *Yamagiri Maru* was found by local divers after a yellowish oil stain was seen by some Trukese boats sailing over the site.

DIVING INFORMATION

THE bow, like the entire shipwreck, is made more difficult to explore because of the ship's orientation on the seabed. It lies at 90 degrees on its port beam. The starboard anchor is out, and its chain leads from the hawse pipe, forward of the bows, and down to the seabed. The bow gun is mounted on a circular platform, and points forward. This piece of ordnance lacks any armour plating, and despite the coral growth, it cuts a stark outline in comparison to the rest of the ship. As one might expect, the shallower sun-filled starboard bow of this ship has become a veritable coral orchard in places. This remains a constant feature throughout the entire starboard beam of the vessel.

Number 1 hold is empty of cargo. Aft of this hold, the diver may find the foremast, cargo winches, and ventilators on the main deck, all pointing out on a line parallel with the seabed. Number 2 hold is also empty of cargo, but is noteworthy because of the bomb damage sustained here. There is a very large sheet of steel that may well have been part of the repair materials in use after the Bismarck Sea incident, for this buckled metal does not appear to correspond to any of the damaged hull plates of the *Yamagiri* in this hold.

Number 3 hold is located aft of the two forward holds, and is raised one deck above main deck level. This slightly smaller hold, though empty of cargo now, would have been serviced by the cargo derricks on the kingpost mast which can be seen at the forward edge of the hold. Like its forward counterpart, this hold is interesting because of the bomb or torpedo damage easily found on the shallower

Opposite: propellor of a
Japanese fighter plane.

starboard side. This may well have been the first hit on the *Yamagiri Maru*, for this is by far the most serious damage on the starboard side, and the vessel was seen by the US pilots to be listing to starboard at the end of the first day of their attack.

The midships superstructure rises majestically four decks higher than Number 3 hold, and the curved frontage of this superstructure now lies across the seabed. Needless to say, all the moveable artefacts in this area of the ship have, like everything else, fallen across the decks down to the seabed. Any search for these artefacts in the silt is likely to be rewarded, but the silt and mud is several feet thick in places. The Dai Nippon beer bottles found on other wrecks in the lagoon are present here too, strewn around the port side of the bridge and cabins below. An engine telegraph remains bolted to the deck of the navigation bridge. It is worth a swim up to the shallower starboard beam here, for there is a coral-encrusted ship's lantern now facing up to the surface. Several rich-coloured soft corals, sponges and anemones also reward such a visit. Aft of the bridge, the huge funnel stretches out from the engineroom beneath it. An examination of the funnel plating will reveal a huge clear letter "Y" fixed to each side. This was the mark of the *Yamagiri*'s owners, the Yamashita Kisen Kaisha line. Also of interest here is the big coral-covered bronze steam whistle attached to the front of the funnel. The funnel is flanked by a ventilator on either side, and some of the lifeboat davits face outboard, while others point inwards.

Exploration deeper inside the cabins of this large wreck is made easier by the wooden partitions and decking having been destroyed by the long fire and wood-boring organisms. Orientation, though, is all the more difficult because of the ship being on its side. Access to the engine room is easy from the aft end of the super-structure. The diver will then see the six huge cylinder blocks in two rows of three. It should be borne in mind though, that whereas wrecks on an even keel have engine rooms well lit by their skylights, the skylights for the *Yamagiri*'s engine room point obstinately towards the gloom of the ocean. Bright, reliable torches are therefore the order of the day here.

Number 4 hold is difficult to enter because of the hatch covers that seal it, but there are two man-sized hatchways through this. This hold may well have been refrigerated, but is reportedly empty of cargo. Moving aft of this hold, the diver will see the aft mast flanked by ventilators. Cargo winches are also in evidence. Rather than the deck dropping one level, it would be more correct to say it is set back one level. This is because the decking is all at right angles to the 35m seabed.

Number 5 hold is generally considered to be the most interesting part of the ship. It is here that the crew of the *Yamagiri* had stowed dozens of huge 18.1in shells for the massive guns of the Japanese battleship *Yamato*. But for the repair-work necessary after the Bismarck Sea incident in 1943, the *Yamagiri* would almost certainly have sailed with the *Yamato* when it left the lagoon after the recon-naissance flight of February 4, 1944. The Japanese battleship *Musashi* was the only other vessel to have these huge guns. These were the largest pieces of naval artillery ever made, and exceeded the largest Allied guns by over two inches. These half-ton live shells, then, are definitely worth a visit, but remember that though these monsters lack fuses, they are live ammunition and their huge explosive charge should be considered unstable. This ordnance can be found in several places around the hold, but they are generally at a depth of 30m. As with everything else in this hold, the warheads are covered in a gossamer layer of silt. It takes very little movement to animate this layer, so photographers are advised to enter before anyone else. As well as these huge projectiles, there are pieces of machinery and metalwork that could well have been for the loading of these shells.

Also in this hold, the diver might find furnaces, boilers, large compressors, and even a steam roller. This vehicle is not intact, but lies at the forward end of the hold. Other finds here include a small bronze propeller, a box of smaller artillery shells, and rows of spade heads. If the wooden shafts were also stowed here then they have since rotted away. Six spoked gun carriage wheels may also be seen.

Number 6 hold is separated from Number 5 by only a small deck house and a couple of ventilators. This hold seems to contain only a cargo of fuel drums, some of which have spilled out across the port side and onto the seabed.

The sterncastle was constructed one deck higher than main deck, and is surrounded by a guard rail that remains largely intact. Securely fixed to the bulkhead is a spare blade of a large propeller. As this does not seem to tally with the *Yamagiri*'s own propeller, it might, like the shells, have been carried for the battleship *Yamato*. Other features of this area include winches, a large transformer, and a great deal of electrical cabling.

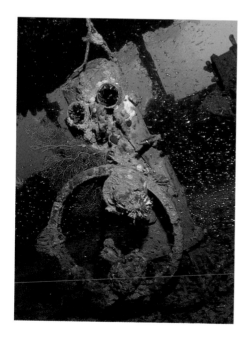

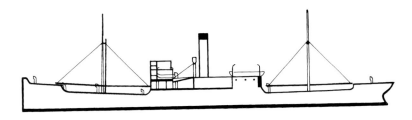

NAME:	YUBAE MARU.
TONNAGE:	3,217.
DIMENSIONS:	93m x 13.4m x 8.2m.
SHIP TYPE:	Steamer.
SUNKEN ATTITUDE:	Lying on port side.
DEPTH TO SEABED:	37m (at bow) 31m (amidships).
DEPTH TO WRECK:	16m (starboard beam).
FEATURES OF NOTE:	Superstructure.

BUILT in 1919, by Ishikawajima Dockyard, the *Yubae*, or *Yubai Maru* had one coal-fired steam engine that could drive the vessel a maximum of 12.3 knots. Pressed into military service on September 22, 1941, it was used as a supply ship for the Imperial Japanese Army. The *Yubae Maru* arrived at Truk in a convoy on February 10, and was attacked and sunk by a 1,000lb bomb and a torpedo, on February 17. It was searched for in the early nineteen-eighties, and eventually found by Gradvin Aisek of the Blue Lagoon Dive Shop in 1983. He had located it merely by noticing a change in colour of the seabed as he drove his boat over it.

DIVING INFORMATION

THE bow is of the plumb design, with some coral growth on and around it. Both the starboard and the port anchors are out, although the port anchor appears to have been blasted from its chain, as either it, or a spare anchor, lies next to a port side mooring cleat on the seabed. Much of the railing around the forecastle remains, as does the big windlass, winch, and take-up drums, used for raising and lowering the anchor. The deck gun and its platform have fallen from their mountings, and now lie partially covered in corals, and half buried in the sand below. Their position suggests that it was the corroding action of the sea, combined with the weight of the artillery piece, that left them where they are today, and not any giant explosions before sinking. Due to the ship's sunken attitude, there is a jumble of assorted metalwork and artefacts along the port sheerstrake.

Exploration of the single forecastle cabin is facilitated by either a doorway on the port side, nearer the sea bed, or a symmetrically positioned equivalent on the shallower starboard side.

Number 1 hold, like all of the ship's five cargo holds, is empty of any real cargo. At least one of the attack photographs of 1944 shows the *Yubae Maru* riding high in the water, which seems to suggest that the ship was empty of cargo during Operation Hailstone. Access from this into Number 2 hold is possible because of the rotting bulkhead that separates the two holds. On shelter deck, the mast, cargo derricks, and winches used to load and unload the cargo are clearly visible. Number 2 hold, like its forward counterpart, contains only some remnants of wooden cargo. It is possible to swim underneath the main deck from this hold, underneath the midships superstructure, and into Number 3 hold. This hold, too, is empty of any cargo.

The bridge area in the two deck levels of midships superstructure is best explored along the seabed, where most of the crew's artefacts are to be found. Finds include the engine telegraph, ship's compass, and an old radio. Most noteable though is the fine collection of crockery bearing a blue leaf design. There are also some plates with the inscription "The Sarawak SS Co. Ltd. Kuching Sarawak" on one side, and "Apsley Pellatte Co. Ltd. 10 Northumberland Ave, Charing Cross, WC" on the reverse. These are apparently destined for the Truk Lagoon museum.

There are passageways aft, on both levels of the superstructure, and also on both port and starboard sides – four in all. Naturally, those on starboard, being shallower and closer to the light, have much more coral growth along them. These coral-laden passageways are quite photogenic.

Aft of the superstructure there is the smaller Number 3 hold, along with the king-post on which the cargo derricks for this hold were mounted. This hold is empty.

Moving further towards the stern, the diver will see that the tall slim smoke stack, characteristic of the old fashioned steamers, has fallen to the seabed. Evidently this item suffered during the bomb bursts that sank the vessel. Aft of where the funnel used to be, there are the engine room skylights. Some of these are open, and offer easy access. As this is one method of gaining entry into the ship's engine room, and another is via Number 4 hold, it makes sense for the diver to use one as entry, and the other for egress, depending on which direction the divers are exploring the shipwreck. The engine room contains a very big steam boiler, whose fire door is open. This maze of catwalks, pipework, steam valves, ladders and gantries is very interesting to explore.

Some of the crew's quarters are located aft of the engine room, and access here is equally as good. The white tiled bathroom is in reasonably good condition. On either side of these deck cabins are the empty lifeboat davits. One sight that makes this wrecksite different from most others in the lagoon, is the presence of a lifeboat, sitting on the seabed, not far from the port davits that carried it. It has rusted badly.

Holds Number 4 and 5 are empty of cargo, but do contain plenty of silt. Between these holds is the aft mast, but this, like much of the decking, and starboard shell plating, shows plenty of damage. This was all caused by the pressure waves of the explosions that sank the *Yubae Maru*.

The sterncastle is one deck above main deck, and here there is a small hold containing varying lengths of chain. Of real interest though is the fascinating steering arrangement for the rudder. A steam engine, positioned on the sterncastle,

Overleaf: inside the fuselage of the Betty bomber.

evidently operated the lengths of chain that run to the rudder, around a big steel wheel, and back again. There are also the remains of two large wheels for operating this chain mechanism by hand. Also of interest next to the rudder is the big four-bladed propeller.

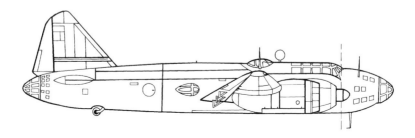

WRECK SITE:	BETTY bomber.
SUNKEN ATTITUDE:	Upright on slight slope.
DEPTH TO SEABED:	14m (at cockpit) 19m (at tail).
DEPTH TO WRECK:	12m (to starboard wing).
FEATURES OF NOTE:	Cockpit, machine guns and radio set.

THE Japanese Mitsubishi G4M long range bomber was designed in 1939 and used all over the Pacific throughout the Second World War. The Allied forces named it the Betty bomber, and it was also nicknamed the Flying Cigar. This was partly an allusion to its uniform cigar-like shape, but was also because the aircraft had unprotected fuel tanks which were regularly hit and set on fire.

The Betty bomber was used to great effect in the attacks and ultimate sinking of the warships HMS *Repulse*, and HMS *Prince of Wales* in the early stages of the war. These tactical bombers were also used in the bombing raids on Darwin in Northern Australia. It was in a Betty bomber too that Admiral Yamamoto was killed when it was shot down by US fighters over Bougainville near the Solomon islands.

Truk Lagoon had Betty bombers on Moen, Param, and Eten airfields. It is not known when this plane crashed, but it was apparently flying in from the north to land on the Eten runway. It appears the nose section and cockpit were badly damaged in the heavy impact with the sea. The shock of this impact, combined with the pulling of the propellers, tore the engines from their mountings. Thus freed, the still rotating propellers drove themselves and the engines a further 100m north east towards Eten runway.

This Betty now lies upright in 11-15m of water, about 135m south west of Eten Island. It is approximately 20m long, and points south. The visibility in this area is worse than in the rest of the lagoon, so photography of this particular wreck is a little more difficult.

DIVING INFORMATION

THE plane's Perspex nose cone was destroyed in the crash, and the pilot's cockpit, aft of this, is badly damaged. Still recognisable though are the metal window frames, and even, in some of these, fragments of Perspex. Finds in this cockpit area include not only the wrecked instrumentation, but also a sake bottle and a bottle of cognac or brandy.

The wings show damage where their engines have torn free, but the aluminium aircraft skin has almost totally resisted the coral colonisation so prevalent on the shallow shipwrecks of Truk. It is therefore possible to make out the ailerons on the wings' trailing edges.

Continuing aft of the cockpit area, the diver will find the remains of the upper observation port. This is also a hatchway that can be used to gain entry or exit from the Betty. Behind the wings, there is an oval shaped gun port on either side of the fuselage. The starboard of these is the easiest to swim through, as the one on port still has some of the original framing and plexiglass. Once inside the bomber, the diver might find the large valve radio set, a fire extinguisher, several boxes, or simply shoals of tiny fish. The rib structure of the aircraft is clearly visible here.

The plane was armed with several guns, and two 7.7mm machine guns, as well as a much larger aerial cannon, may be found on the seabed near the fuselage. This latter piece of ordnance may well have come from the tail gunner's position.

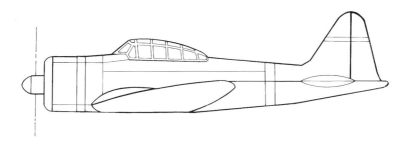

WRECK SITE:	ZERO fighter (NE Eten Island).
SUNKEN ATTITUDE:	Upside down.
DEPTH TO SEABED:	2m.
DEPTH TO WRECK:	1m.
FEATURES OF NOTE:	Cannons on wings, and deployed undercarriage.

THE Mitsubishi A6M Reisen or Zero was a single-seater, single-engined Japanese fighter. Although it was a deservedly feared plane by the Allies in the beginning of the war, its lack of armour protection for either pilot or fuel tank made it vulnerable to the slightly more advanced Allied fighters that were being used later on. As the more advanced, heavier armoured, A6M5b Zero was not used until June and July 1944, it is doubtful any of these models were ever used in Truk.

DIVING INFORMATION

OF all the aircraft wrecks currently known about in Truk, this one has the most coral growth on it. To say it lies in shallow water is an understatement, as one of its propeller blades sticks out of the water. Whereas in other countries this would mean that it would soon be completely broken up by waves, here in Truk the plane has been protected by the surrounding islands and reef, as well as by law.

The dive boats usually have to pay a mooring fee to the nearby local fisherman or his family, and this is often paid by the diver as opposed to the tour operator. However, at only around $5, and as there are two aircraft wrecks to explore, not to mention the north part of Eten Island, this is well worth paying.

The heavy coral growth combined with the two heavy calibre wing mounted cannons of this plane have led to several conflicting identifications. If it is not one of the later models of Zero, then it could be a Tojo fighter.

WRECK SITE:	ZERO fighter (north of southernmost tip of Eten Island).
SUNKEN ATTITUDE:	Upside down.
DEPTH TO SEABED:	9m.
DEPTH TO WRECK:	7m.
FEATURES OF NOTE:	Engine and undercarriage.

DUE to the fairly extensive damage to the bodywork of this fighter, and the fact that it is upside down, it is reasonable to assume its angle of entry into the water, and its impact speed were both very high. This, and the bullet holes, then give credence to the theory that it was shot down from altitude. As the plane dived out of control, it appears to have crashed into the sea upside down.

DIVING INFORMATION

IT IS comparatively easy to snorkel down to this wreck, although it is far more comfortable to use a scuba set. The cylinder does not of course have to be full, and many divers might find they have 80-100 bars left after their first dive. This may be insufficient for a full second dive, but ideal for five minutes or so around shallow sites such as this, bottom time permitting.

The aluminium aircraft skin has largely resisted any attempt of coral to grow on it, which means there is more for the diver to see. The cockpit is very difficult to get to because the Zero is upside down, but everything else is easy to photograph and examine.

WRECK SITE:	ZERO fighter (west of Param Island).
SUNKEN ATTITUDE:	Broken into three sections.
DEPTH TO SEABED:	15m.
DEPTH TO WRECK:	14m.

DIVING INFORMATION

THE wreckage of this plane is located about 450m west of the shallow junkyard off Param Island. It has been reported as having broken into three sections – the engine, the cockpit port wing and fuselage, and the tail section. From its position, it has been deduced that it was taking off from the Param runway when it was apparently shot down.

The radial engine can be found 50m away from the wreck, and seems to have driven itself further along the sandy seabed to its present position.

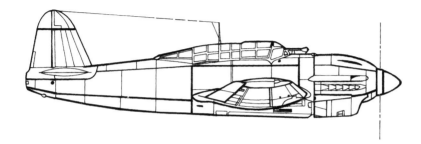

WRECK SITE:	JUDY dive bomber (NE Eten Island).
SUNKEN ATTITUDE:	Upright.
DEPTH TO SEABED:	3m.
DEPTH TO WRECK:	2m.
FEATURES OF NOTE:	Cockpit, bullet holes in fuselage.

THE Yokosuka D4Y Suisei or Comet, was named the "Judy" dive bomber by the Allied forces. Originally developed from the German Heinkel He 118V4, the earliest Judy dive bombers were even powered by imported Daimler Benz engines. The design progressed, and the Judy dive bombers became the fastest carrier-based fighters of the entire war. Towards the end of hostilities, it was even adapted for a night-fighting role. As well as operating from carriers, Judy bombers could just as easily be based on land, as they were in Truk.

This Judy dive bomber evidently crashed after take-off. Its single Aichi Kokuki-built engine would have been at full throttle as the airplane was shot down. The plane's impact with the water, along with the high revs of its propeller, meant that the engine tore itself loose from its mountings and the rest of the airframe. The still-rotating propeller then drove the engine further along the seabed than the rest of the aircraft. The increased resistance of the tail plane then dragged it away from the more streamlined fuselage. This left the Judy dive bomber in three large sections about 100m north-east of Eten Island.

DIVING INFORMATION

THE two-man Judy dive bomber lies near a Zero fighter in very shallow water. It is easy to snorkel over this wreck and take photographs. As with the other planes nearby, there is not a great deal of coral growth on the aluminium skin. This makes it much easier to find the neat, round, bullet holes responsible for destroying the controls, or killing the pilot. These can be found on the wings as well as the fuselage.

The cockpit is covered by the arched metal frames that held the plexiglass, some of which remains intact. This portion of the wreck supports more coral growth than the rest of the plane. For this reason the controls and instruments are largely obscured. The engine would have been mounted immediately in front of this cockpit, although there is only a tangle of pipes, cables, and shorn bolts there now. Geared cogs can be found in front of the plane, and seem to point to where the engine now lies.

The tail section is, apart from having broken away from the rest of the fuselage, in remarkable condition. Like the rest of the aircraft the metal skin appears to be a gold colour.

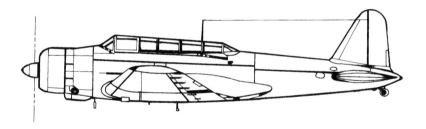

WRECK SITE:	KATE torpedo bomber (north of Eten).
SUNKEN ATTITUDE:	Upright.
DEPTH TO SEABED:	34-35m.
DEPTH TO WRECK:	33m.
FEATURES OF NOTE:	Cockpit, rear machine gun, and bullet holes in fuselage.

THE Nakajima B5N was developed as a carrier-based bomber. A single-engined three-seater aircraft, it was in production from 1936-43. The "Kate", as the Allies named it, was built at Koizumi, Nagoya, and Hiro. They were torpedo bombers, and capable of carrying a single 800kg torpedo, or its equivalent in bombs. More than 1,000 were built in the eight years they were in production, and 144 of these were reportedly used in the attack on Pearl Harbour in 1941.

The Kate bomber was also responsible for sinking the three US carriers *Lexington, Yorktown* and *Hornet.* This fast bomber of German design was superceded by the Nakajima B6N or "Jill" because the Kate had very poor protection for its fuel tanks, and little armour for its crew of pilot, observer-bomb aimer, and radio operator-rear gunner. It was however not made obsolete. The Kate was used instead for reconnaissance or anti-submarine warfare.

This particular wreck was discovered by the crew of the *Thorfinn* in the latter part of 1988.

DIVING INFORMATION

THIS Kate torpedo bomber apparently lies upright on a gently sloping bottom of between 33m-35m. It lies in the middle of the channel between Dublon and Eten islands. It is reported to be in pristine condition. Noted features of this plane include the instrument panel and the control column. The rear-facing machine gun is also reported to be on its mounting, and there are reports too of a number of bullet holes in the fuselage.

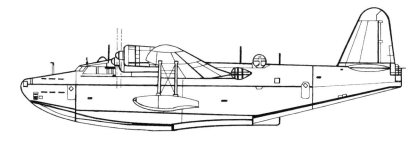

WRECK SITE:	EMILY flying boat H8K2
SUNKEN ATTITUDE:	Upside down.
DEPTH TO SEABED:	15m.
DEPTH TO WRECK:	12m.
FEATURES OF NOTE:	Cockpit, four engines and wing floats.

THE Kawanishi H6K was designed by the Japanese in 1938, to carry out long-range reconnaissance and bombing raids. It was fitted with two large engines on each wing, and these gave the big plane a maximum speed of 276 mph. The aircraft had a maximum range of 4,500 nautical miles, and was armed with 20mm cannons. The "Emily", as the Allied forces named the plane, could also be fitted with two wing mounted torpedoes, or eight 551lb bombs, or even sixteen 132lb bombs/depth charges.

The Emily flying boat was used by the Japanese on one noteworthy raid of Honolulu in March, 1942. Two of the planes took off from Wotje in the eastern Marshall islands and headed for their target island of Oahu. Including the refuelling stop by submarines at French Frigate Shoals (to the north-west of the Hawaiian islands), this made a round trip of over 4,860 statute miles. The planes carried out their bombing mission, but because of the low cloud many of the bombs missed the city.

This particular Emily could have been attached to the seaplane base on Dublon, or it might have stopped off for refuelling, or even an emergency landing. There is some confusion about exactly how this Emily sank, but it is reasonable to assume that it was landing when either it hit a very large obstacle, or if the hull was damaged, it suddenly took in a great deal of water.

Accepting this as a plausible chain of events, there is reason to believe that this is actually the Emily that was forced to crash land at Truk after having been attacked by US fighters. Vice Admiral Hara and his Chief of Staff, along with several other officers, had apparently taken this flight with the intention of getting to Palau for a high-level military conference. The flight was intercepted by US fighters, and despite heavy resistance by the Emily's gunners took a great deal of damage. Apparently there were several fatalities inside the aircraft, including the co-pilot and some of Hara's staff. After climbing to 30,000 feet the pilot could still not shake off the attackers, and it was only when he later found large cloud formations that he was able to evade the pursuers. The aircraft made it back to Truk, but is reported to have crashed during the landing. Vice Admiral Hara survived, and the pilot was duly decorated.

DIVING INFORMATION

THE Emily lies upside-down in 15m of water. The aircraft has broken into three sections, and coral growth is generally light. The plane's boat-like hull can easily be seen, as can the wing-mounted sponsons or floats. The large nose area has broken up, but the lower observation ports used to survey beneath the aircraft can be clearly made out. The cockpit and all the flight instruments are now underneath the wreckage on the seabed, but it is possible to enter the fuselage either at the front or through a break towards the tail.

All four engines remain intact, with some colourful sponge growth on the propellers. The sponson mounted on the plane's port wing has become detached, but is basically intact. This compares quite dramatically to the starboard sponson which evidently bore the brunt of the landing once the hull had taken in the water and settled lower. This float has been severely dented from the heavy landing.

The aft section of the aircraft contains the tail and tail planes and the remains of the tail gunner's postion. It is where this tail section has broken away from the rest of the fuselage that divers may enter the Emily. Finds here include a radio set.

WRECK SITE:	Dumping Ground.
DEPTH TO SEABED:	26m.
DEPTH TO WRECK:	24m.
FEATURES OF NOTE:	Half track personnel carriers
	and Japanese staff car.

DIVING INFORMATION

IN THE sea passage between Dublon and Fefan islands, at a depth of 26m, is a collection of six assorted military tracked and half-tracked vehicles, a mulititude of aircraft parts and bodywork, as well as what is reported to have been Vice Admiral Hara's own personal staff car. A few lorries, two propellers, and many torpedoes as well as torpedo parts may also be found among the coils of cabling and other rubbish. All these vehicles were apparently cleared off the islands by the Japanese and taken to this dumping ground by barge. The barge apparently jettisoned all these vehicles at or near a buoy that can now be seen on the sea bed.

The restored standard dress diving helmet seen at the Blue Lagoon Dive Shop was found here, and there is speculation that there are more to be found.

INFORMATION FOR TRAVELLERS

C HUUK state, or Truk Lagoon, consists of 290 islands and islets with a land area of 127 sq km (49 sq miles). Fringed with mangrove swamps, the seven larger volcanic islands of Truk Lagoon then rise from sea level to the populated grassy slopes through scrub, and up to the tropical rainforests on the mountainous areas of the interior. The climate throughout the Federated States of Micronesia is tropical. The area has a high humidity of around 80 per cent with an average rainfall of about 3,000 millimetres (120 inches). Cloudy days might come as a shock to any European tourists with pre-conceived ideas of endless Pacific sunshine, but it is as well to remember that Truk's climate does support a rainforest. Temperatures remain constant at around 27-30°C. Sea temperatures also remain constant at around 28°C: so there is little need for much thermal protection while diving there. The small land masses maintain such an agreeable climate, because the cooling sea breezes prevent any excessive temperatures or humidity. The most pleasant time to visit is between November and April; and while it is certainly still inviting from May to October, this period can be called the islands' wet season.

The four Federated States of Micronesia (Pohnpei, Kosrae, Yap, and Chuuk), have a combined population of 105,000 (1989), with a projection of 128,000 by the year 2000. Forty four per cent of the population live in Chuuk State (Truk Lagoon). Of these, 14,218 live on Moen island.

There is no official language, as each island group has its own language. Trukese is the local language, but English is spoken almost everywhere, so there is little need to panic if you are unable to find a Trukese-English dictionary in the shops. Not surprisingly, bearing in mind the islands' history, Japanese is also spoken, although this tends to be by the older generations. Japanese tourists are conspicuous by their absence in Truk.

There is no official religion either, but Christianity is widely practised. With the sole exception of the predominantly Roman Catholic Yap islands, the states are predominantly Protestant. Sunday services are characteristically lively affairs, full of vibrancy and Pacific island music. These services bear little resemblance to the generally more conservative approach of our European churches, and a visit is recommended.

CURRENCY

THE accepted currency of the islands is the US dollar and travellers' cheque. Unlike some countries which require a declaration of the importation of large sums of money, there is no limit to the import or export of foreign or local currency. It should, however, be borne in mind that foreign exchange facilities are limited. As in the States, you will find that US dollar travellers' cheques are generally accepted as cash, provided they have the change for the denomination you are offering. Credit cards that are generally accepted are Access/Mastercard, and Visa, but it is wise to check with your credit card company for details of merchant acceptability before your trip. Some of the dive operators do not accept credit cards. Banks are open from 10.00 to 15.00 Monday to Thursday, and 10.00 to 18.00 on Friday, so be careful when budgeting, because it is unlikely that divers will return to Moen, which has the only banking in Truk, before about 16.00 each day. Normal office hours are 10.00 to 13.00 Monday to Friday, and shopping hours are 08:00 to 21:00 Monday to Saturday.

Bank of the Federated States of Micronesia, PO Box 640, Moen, Truk, FSM 96942. Tel: 330-2353/4/5. Telex: 729-6847. Open from 09:30-14:30 Monday to Friday.

Bank of Guam, P.O. Box 69, Moen, Truk, FSM 96942. Tel: 330-2331 & 330-2567. Telex: 729-6837. Open from 10:00-15:00 Monday to Thursday. Open from 10:00-17:00 Friday.

ELECTRICITY

ELECTRICITY is only found on the major islands, is notoriously intermittent, and is susceptible to power failures during the fairly frequent tropical rain storms. It is 110/120 volts AC (60 cycles). Truk uses the two-pin US plug and sockets system, so suitable adaptors are required if travellers are taking any European electrical appliances with them. The alternative is to fit US plugs on everything you intend to use. A stopover in Hawaii or Guam en route to Truk Lagoon would enable you to buy any suitable items like US plugs, battery chargers for your flash guns etc. These places are also ideal for collecting the luxury items that are in short supply in the few Trukese shops. Tourism is still in its infancy in the major islands of the Federated States of Micronesia, and virtually non-existent on the smaller islands.

TIME DIFFERENCES

TRUK is 11 hours ahead of Greenwich mean time, and if European travellers approach from the US they should remember that when crossing the dateline from the east, the date is increased by one. Subsequently, if travellers leave Truk, and head East towards the US, then the date is decreased by one. The Northern Mariana Islands are 10 hours ahead of GMT; Pohnpei Island is 11 hours ahead; and the Marshall Islands and Palau 12 hours ahead.

TRAVEL

MOEN has an International Airport (TKK) which consists of only one airstrip, and a couple of airport buildings. This is located only 2km from the business centre of Chuuk State. There is currently only one airline flying in and out of Truk, and that is the American Continental Airlines. There are only three or four flights a week, and they are from Hawaii or Guam. They also fly to Pohnpei and Yap. Travellers will usually have at least one, but more likely two or three stop-overs before reaching the atoll, so there is little likelihood of suffering jet lag immediately on arriving in the islands. A word of warning here is that the space for cabin luggage is at a premium on some of these flights, so divers with bulging bags of gauges, pressure-sensitive diving computers, depth gauges and camera equipment are advised to seek the help of cabin staff. They are very helpful in finding spaces around the plane for your bags.

Nauru Pacific Shipping Lines provides a passenger service from Honolulu to Truk and Pohnpei for the traveller with more time to spare.

Visas are required by all visitors (with the exception of US citizens) intending to stay longer than 30 days. The stipulations for any visit are that you show proof of a return ticket, adequate funds for your stay, and a passport valid for at least 60 days beyond your date of entry. A British Visitor's passport would not be accepted.

There are two types of visa: tourist, and employment. Should visitors be planning a stay of 30 days or more, then application should be made to: The Chief of Immigration, Federated States of Micronesia, Kolonia, Pohnpei EC1 96941. Tel: 606/604.

This office is open from 08.00-17.00 during weekdays. It should be remembered that each of the four constitutional governments of Micronesia is responsible for its own tourism policies, and should tourists be planning visits to any of the island groups outside the Federated States of Micronesia, then they should make the relevant enquiries for visa requirements with their travel agents.

ISLAND TRANSPORT

LAND taxis are a ridiculously cheap yet efficient form of transport. These take the form of a pick-up truck with a cardboard or other rudimentary sign in the windscreen announcing "Taxi". The cost is currently 25 cents, or 50 cents if travelling to either the southern extremity of Moen (The Continental Hotel), or the Eastern extremity, (Sapuk). You tell the driver where you would like to go, then join your co-travellers in the back of the pick-up. Some taxis have a few stools or wooden benches to sit on, but judging by the way these slide about when rounding corners, I am not sure whether they actually add to your comfort. The driver will then continue his drive around Moen, depositing and collecting passengers as he goes. Punctuality is measured on a more geological scale in Truk than in the west, so don't be alarmed if your driver goes in the opposite direction to the one you requested. He is merely dropping someone else off before he follows in your vague direction.

When the taxi driver has had enough of cruising around Moen, he will merely remove the cardboard sign and revert to being a private vehicle. All is not sweetness and roses though, for all Trukese taxis disappear from the roads at 1630; you will not get a taxi for love nor money after that hour. Believe me, I tried.

The alternative is to hire a car, or, if you are a resident of the Continental Hotel, you also have the option of hiring an attractively-coloured scooter, which is perfect for exploring the island.

Four Car Rental firms currently operating in Truk are:

Bernie's Car Rental: PO Box 153, Moen, Truk 96942. Tel: (691) 330-2677.

Jerry Car Rental: PO Box 160, Moen, Truk 96942. Tel: (691) 330-2487. Telex: 6840.

J & R Rent-A-Car: PO Box 934, Moen, Truk 96942. Tel: (691) 330-2215.

V.J. Car Rental: The Christopher Inn, Moen, Truk 96942. Tel: (691) 330-2652.

Prices for car hire will inevitably vary, and increase with any inflation, and a 10 per cent tax is often levied. The daily cost is currently around $40-$50 a day.

For inter-island transportation within Truk Lagoon itself, there are excellent water taxis operating, primarily for the locals from the market and docks on Moen. This area is on the north-west side of the island, approximately 1.5km south of the airport terminal.

The Truk Shipping Company (Box 669, Moen, Truk 96942. Tel: 330-2455) offers a means of transport to other nearby island groups such as the fascinating Western Islands, or the Upper and Lower Mortlocks. Ships only travel every two weeks or so, and the trip lasts about one week. There are two types of ticket available – deck and cabin. However, due to the infrequency of the ships, these often go quickly. Trips to the nearby Upper Mortlocks can also be made by the Government boats which travel twice a week.

PUBLIC HOLIDAYS
Public Holidays in Truk are as follows:

Jan 1	New Year's Day.		
Jan 20	Martin Luther King's Birthday.		
Feb 18	President's Day.		
May 10	Federated States of Micronesia Constitution Day.		
May 27	Memorial Day.		
Jul 4	Independence Day.		
Jul 12	Micronesian Day.		
Sep 2	Labour Day.		
Sep 23	Charter Day.		
Oct 11	Veterans' Day.		
Oct 12	Columbus' Day.		
Nov 1	All Saints' Day.		
Nov 2	All Souls' Day.	Nov 28	Thanksgiving Day.
Nov 11	Veterans' Day.	Dec 25	Christmas Day.

COMMUNICATIONS

COMMUNICATIONS are generally good, but to date there is no international direct dialling. All such phone calls have to be made through the international operator, and there are no problems in making such calls at either of the two larger hotels, or the FSM Telecommunication Centre on Moen. There are no public pay-phones on the islands, and only one person in 60 in the archipelago owns a telephone.

Telex machines are available at the government communications office, and air mail to the UK takes at least ten days. The Post Office on Moen is open from 07.30 to 14.30, and deals with island stamps (which tend to make nice souvenirs as well as collector's items). They will also insure your mail, and deal with registering if so desired. There are television and radio stations in Truk, although the services are very limited.

ENTERTAINMENT

AS Truk is dry state, and there are no bars or pubs for the islanders, the usual form of evening entertainment for tourists takes the form of drinks or video shows in one of the hotels. In the case of The Continental hotel, there is generally a good programme of diving-related videos in the evening. This takes place in one of the restaurants. Each show is well advertised throughout the hotel.

Nightlife is restricted, with a few exceptions, to the Hotels on Moen. As a tourist, the visitor can make an application for an Alcoholic Beverage Consumption Licence at the Police station on Moen, if he wishes to drink outside the hotels. Drinking in public is, as in the US, strictly prohibited, but American beers are available "under the counter" at various establishments throughout Truk. Almost any local would be happy to tell you where they are, and the police tend to turn a blind eye to this practice as long as it is not a blatant transgression of the laws. There are also what are termed "government picnics". These are basically parties held on the uninhabited islands of the lagoon to get around the restrictive alcohol rules on the other islands.

FOOD

LOCAL specialities are breadfruit, and thin slices of fish dipped in a peppery sauce. It is also possible to enjoy the equally exotic tastes of other cultures while on Moen.

The Seaside Restaurant: Japanese food. (Opposite the Bank of Guam and Susumu's store).

Yumi's Restaurant: Filipino food. (Opposite the airport).

Join Us Coffee Shop: Korean food (Near the airport).

Ran Annim Restaurant: US-style (Near the airport).

Heryo's and Sons Restaurant: US-style (Behind Ran Annim's).

It is possible to go on fishing trips while not diving, and visitors may expect to catch wahoo, yellow fin mackerel, bonito, and sea bass. These catches will then likely be cooked and prepared for you by your hotel, for your evening meal.

ACCOMMODATION

THERE are two hotels on Moen, but other accommodation is available. Due to the popularity of the islands with divers and other visitors, it is strongly advisable to book rooms in advance of your stay.

The Continental Hotel, PO Box 340, Moen, Truk, FSM 96942.
Tel: (691) 330-2727 & 330-2438. Fax: 330-2439.

Tucked away in a delightful grove of coconut palms on the south-west corner of the island, remote from the town in the north, the Continental Hotel is the state's foremost hotel. Each of its 56 rooms has a balcony, offering views of the coconut groves and the sea. There are two restaurants, volley ball courts, a beach bar, a gift shop and sports equipment rental. The hotel offers a laundry service, and visitors can also hire the hotel's scooters. It has its own jetty, from which dive boats will collect you and your dive kit each morning. Divers returning from their day trip will find the fresh-water shower on the jetty useful, and the beach bar temptingly close.

The hotel is built on and near the remains of the sea plane base that was so comprehensively attacked in the last war. It is therefore possible to explore the hotel's surroundings, and discover remains of an assortment of buildings and defensive structures.

Prices will of course vary seasonally, but visitors can expect to pay around $90-100 dollars a night.

The Christopher Inn, PO Box 37, Moen, Truk, FSM 96942.
Tel: (691) 330-2652.

Conveniently situated near the airport and shopping centre of Moen, visitors will find the 31 rooms of this hotel comfortable and less expensive than those of the Continental. Air conditioning and en suite showers can be found in most rooms, and cheaper rooms, with ceiling fans rather than air conditioning, are available. The hotel has a very reasonable roof garden bar and restaurant and also boasts a conference room. Divers can order packed lunches from the restaurant, and pick them up an hour later. The hotel offers a free bus service to and from the airport, and cars may also be hired by the day. As a smaller, family-run hotel, comparisons should not be made with the more exotic Continental. The Christopher Inn does, however, have a friendly atmosphere, and is a more economical place to stay (around $45.00 a night).

The Tradewind Hotel, PO Box 520, Mechitiu, Moen, Truk, FSM 96942.
Tel: (691) 330-2781.

Self-catering apartments with air conditioning. Located 2km away from the airport on the north coast road. Rooms $50-60.

Falos Beach Resort, PO Box 494, Falos, Truk, FSM 96942.
Tel: (691) 330-2606. Telex: 6831 Falos. Fax: 330-2706.

Seven tin-roofed bungalows on a small island 25 minutes' boat ride away from Moen (to the north). The cost for one of these is around $45-55 per night. Elementary provisions are available from a small shop on the island, as well as barbeque pits, and picnic shelters. Snorkelling equipment is also available for hire. The island has running water, but visitors should expept certain restrictions. It is however a beautiful island, and, many would say, worth the sacrifices.

Truk Stop, PO Box 546, Moen, Truk, FSM 96942.
Tel: (691) 330-2701. Fax: 2286.
 Four rooms with kitchen facilities are available at a cost of $55 each. Car hire is also available.

Ace, PO Box 369, Moen, Truk, FSM 96942.
Tel: (691) 330-2580.
 Three self-catering apartments.

Seaside, PO Box 100, Moen, Truk, FSM 96942.
Tel: (691) 330-2445. Telex: 6831. Fax: 330-2445.
 Four self-catering apartments near shops and a restaurant.

HEALTH
TRUK has a recompression chamber in the State Hospital on Moen.
 Visitors are advised to take innoculations against typhoid, polio, tetanus and cholera. The risk of infection from food or water in a hotel is minimal, but many visitors choose to drink only bottled water, and to have no ice cubes unless they are made from such water. There have been outbreaks of cholera, but the high-risk areas tend to be off the tourist routes. If you go camping in some of the more remote islands, then you are advised to purify all water with tablets or iodine beforehand.
 Due to the maritime influence, there is no risk of malaria.
 If visitors arrive from a yellow fever infected country, they will be required to produce evidence of innoculation against that disease.
 Milk is pasteurised, and all dairy products are considered safe for consumption, as are the local meat, vegetable, fruit, and seafoods. One dish of uncooked reef-fish however, called sashimi, has been the culprit of some upsets, and should therefore be avoided.
 Health insurance is likely to be expensive for divers, but is still recommended. Some travellers even like to take their own supply of hypodermic needles (in case they require a course of treatment from a small hospital). Divers should take the usual warm-water precautions against ear infections.

DIVING COMPANIES
THERE are currently five diving companies operating in Truk and these companies are responsible for collecting the payment for each visitor's diving permit. This permit costs only a few dollars.

The Blue Lagoon Dive Shop, PO Box 429, Moen, Truk, FSM 96942
Tel: (691) 330-2796

Owned by Kimiuo Aisek, this is the oldest and most respected diving operator in Truk Lagoon. At the age of 17 Kimiuo watched the Japanese ships being bombed and torpedoed by the American fighter-bombers in Operation Hailstone. In 1969, he led Jacques Cousteau to many of the wrecks, and in subsequent years he and his eldest son Gradvin have been responsible for locating many more of the "lost" ships. Blue Lagoon Dive Shop runs seven dive boats, each equipped with two engines. They have 250 cylinders, 3,000 weights for 50 weight belts, and 18 employees. The operation can ably cater for 60 divers per day, and groups larger than five get a discount at the rate of 7 per cent. All of the diving equipment required can be hired from the company.

BLDS charges $65 per day per diver for two cylinders, weights and weight belt, and use of a dive guide and dive boat. Other equipment can be hired.

A popular aspect of this company's operation is the fact that they have no restrictions on what wrecks they will dive. Provided the visitor can show adequate qualifications and experience at the target depth, even wrecks like the *Aikoku Maru* and the *San Francisco Maru* can be dived.

Because of the inevitable popularity of this family business, divers are advised to book places in advance, as BLDS can on occasion be fully booked.

Micronesia Aquatics, PO Box 57, Moen, Truk, FSM 96942
Tel: (691) 330-2204. Telex: 6831. Fax: 330-2204.

Owned by Clark and Chineina Graham, Micronesia Aquatics are based in the grounds of the Continental Hotel. Dives are charged at the rate of $65 per day per person. This includes two cylinders, weights and weight belt, and the use of a dive guide plus boat. An additional dive may be made at a cost of $25. Divers should bring their own basic equipment as well as bouyancy devices, demand valves, and contents pressure gauge. There is however some equipment available for hire.

Micronesia Aquatics have three dive boats and three dive masters.

As well as diving, Micronesia Aquatic also offers snorkelling trips ($30), trips on a glass-bottomed boat ($25 for three hours), rental of windsurfing equipment ($10 an hour), and water-skiing.

Ghost Fleet Dive Shop, PO Box 295, Moen, Truk, FSM 96942.
Tel: (691) 330-2724. Telex: 6831.

This operation is run by Rochy Luther, and can be found just outside the Continental Hotel in a large pink building with a large US-style diver's flag painted on one side.

Truk Scuba Dive Centre, PO Box 747, Moen, Truk, FSM 96942.
Tel: (691) 330-2547.

This operation is run by Hans Wiliander.

S.S. Thorfinn (live-aboard ship), PO Box DX, Weno, Moen, Truk, FSM 96942. Tel: (691) 330-4302. Fax: (691) 330-4253.

Run by Captain Lance Higgs, this 52m-long ship has 13 double cabins, each with its own sink. The showers and toilets on each deck serve all of the cabins on that deck. Passengers have the use of E6 film processing. There are four 7.3m twin-engined doreys to take divers to four different sites each day.

Truk Aggressor (live-aboard ship), PO Box 70, Weno, Moen, Truk, FSM 96942. Contact: Charly Anerson.

This vessel is the most recent live-aboard dive boat in Truk and measures 36.5m in length with a beam of 8.2m. It has a cruising speed of 14 knots, and a potential range of 5,000 miles. The fresh water storage holds 7,000 gallons, and the boat has the facility to make 1,200 gallons more each day. There are ten double air conditioned staterooms, each with its own private toilet and shower. There is also a large saloon with bar and audio-visual facilities. The video editing suite has been designed to help divers get the most from their underwater footage, and for stills photographers, there are also the crucial E6 film developing facilities. On deck there is a spacious 14m x 8m sun deck, complete with bar buffet and barbeque.

On the diving side of the operation is a large 5m x 3m diving platform at the stern of the ship. This is low in the water with two sets of steps and handrails offering easy exit for the fully-kitted diver. There are two fresh-water showers here, and ample room for hanging wetsuits and storing dive kit. Here too there is a sun-shaded area on either side of the ship. The 48 diving cylinders can be charged from two Mako 5,000psi compressors, and there are also two inflatable boats used as dive tenders.

Of the seven Aggressor dive-boats worldwide, this is the latest and the most luxuriously appointed.

OTHER ATTRACTIONS
FOLLOWING the League of Nations Mandate, when Japan gained control of Truk Lagoon, they named Moen Haru Shima, meaning spring. Moen is now the commercial centre of Chuuk State. All the diving operators offer trips to underwater sites here, and there are several land sites worth visiting.

Near the state hospital, under the Vinifauren Ridge, is a small cave system hewn from the rock. Walking along the low tunnel, the visitor soon arrives at a gun emplacement and large gun, with fine views over the west coast of Moen. Access to this emplacement is gained by driving past the hospital and continuing on to a large green water tank. There is a small area to park cars here, and an overgrown footpath then leads up the hillside through the heavy foliage to the gun emplacement.

Other sites of interest include the spectacular views from the top of Mt Tonachau near the airport, and the pretty Wichon Falls and swimming hole.

Driving further east along this north road, the visitor cannot fail to notice the other wrecks of Truk Lagoon. These are the cars, pick-up trucks, and vans which have been left to the jungle on both sides of the road. Continuing on to the areas of Penia then Sapuk, tourists will find Xavier High School, then the Japanese lighthouse and another gun emplacement. The heavy metal hatches, and substantial reinforced concrete walls betray the fact that the High School was once the fortified Japanese radio communications centre. Having been bought by the Jesuits, this is now one of the finest schools in Micronesia.

Access to the old Japanese lighthouse is made difficult by the amount of jungle which threatens to swamp it, as well as the number of locals who claim ownership, and therefore a fee from each visitor. It is located on the highest point of the Sapuk peninsular, but the views from this bullet-pock-marked building are worth the trouble. Below the lighthouse at the bottom of the north-east slope, you will also find the large gun emplacement, with its Italian guns still pointing stubbornly towards the Northeast Pass.

There is currently no road going right around the island, and some of the road on the south-east coast is very rough indeed. Any visitor intrepid enough to walk around the Mt Witpan area will be rewarded by Moen's third mountaintop gun emplacement. A guide, though, is recommended.

Near the hospital, down a dead-end road, in someone's private garden, there is also the overgrown wreck of a Nakajima reconnaissance plane. The ground is boggy, and the owner must of course be consulted before any visitors walk over to it.

Eten's Japanese name was Takeshima, meaning bamboo. A fighter, and fighter-bomber airfield during the Second World War, many of the island's ruins are being overgrown by the verdant bush growth. The island is just over 1,000m long, with much of that once used by a single airstrip. Patches of the tarmac runway may still be found among the coconut palms, and colourful wild flowers almost conceal the concrete buildings so devasted by the 500lb and 1,000lb bombs dropped by the US forces. Some of the buildings are being used for the local production of copra from dried coconuts, and others are used by the islanders as homes. The huge two- and three-storey concrete structures have all but collapsed on one side, and the heavy steel doors are clearly pock-marked by large armour-piercing cannon shells.

Originally called Toloas, Dublon was, in 1814, named after Manuel Dublon, who was a Spaniard collecting Beche de Mer for trade. Under German rule in the late 19th century, the island and its people then came under Japanese control after the First World War. The Japanese then named the island Natsu Shima, meaning summer. Dublon was once the main island for Truk Lagoon, but with so many Japanese soldiers and sailors having been taken prisoner here after the Second World War, the US forces were obliged to use another island as their base from which they could administer the atoll. The island they chose was Moen, which is the reason that Moen and not Dublon, is now the political, financial, and commercial centre of Chuuk State.

On the south coast of Dublon, looking out onto nearby Eten Island, is the huge sea plane base that was so comprehensively attacked during Operation Hailstone. Many of the slipways and ramps into the water remain, as do the concrete bomb shelters. Near this old airfield is a track leading up the steep slopes of Mt Tonomwan to yet another of Truk's defences. The jungle growth here necessitates the use of a guide to find this site, but again the views from these heights make it all worthwhile. It was this gun emplacement that gave the American pilots so much trouble during the second day of Operation Hailstone. The AA fire from the Japanese gunners at this post reportedly improved quite noticeably, according to the attack reports.

A cave system and network of tunnels known as the General's Cave can be found in the middle of Dublon. Further along the road from the Japanese naval cemetry, this cave is still used by locals as a typhoon shelter. If visitors wish to explore it properly, a torch is required.

Most of the island activity in the war was on the south-west peninsula of Dublon. Now overgrown by luxuriant bushes and trees, sites here include the big oil-storage tanks for the Japanese Imperial Navy, the Japanese Governor's residence, and another gun emplacement.

The Japanese named Fefan island Akishima, meaning autumn. Apart from the sites of military interest, which include an overgrown gun emplacement on the higher slopes, and three field guns north of Mesa Wharf, Fefan is also of interest for its market of handicrafts. Visitors to Truk may be able to find the lovesticks characteristic of the original culture, the Tapuanu masks, war clubs or even shark-tooth knuckle-dusters!

Between the islands of Fefan and Udot, the small island of Param had one of Truk's five airfields, and was comprehensively bombed during Operation Hailstone. The aircraft that were unusable after this attack were simply pushed off the end of the runway into the sea. For a nominal landing fee, visitors can explore the ruins of this old airfield, and still see the shot-up remains of many aircraft lying in shallow water on the south-west shore. Derelict mines also litter the beaches here.

Suiyo To, or Wednesday, as Tol island was called by the Japanese, is now actually three smaller islands. Once the largest island of the lagoon, the Japanese military forced locals to dig channels through the narrower parts of Tol so that their patrol boats did not have to take long detours around the large peninsulars. As with many of the other islands in Truk, this one is edged by a great deal of mangrove swamp. These swamps have their own peculiar wildlife, such as the mudskippers and fiddler crabs, and are interesting places to visit. One rare animal worth tracking down is the large and ferocious looking land crab. This creature has become a delicacy with the Trukese, and can sometimes be seen scaling palm trees to cut down its own coconuts.

Tol is geographically more separated from the commercial centre of Truk, and nearly became a separate state on its own, but this move was stopped by presidential veto.

The Piaanu Pass, to the west of Tol, is protected by four large pieces of artillery. These two pairs of guns can be found in two impressive caves on the western-most tip of Polle island.

USEFUL ADDRESSES
SOME useful addresses for visitors to Truk are:

Truk Visitors Bureau, PO Box FQ, Moen, Truk, FSM 96942.
Tel: (691) 303-4133. Fax: (691) 303-2777.

Truk Travel Services, PO Box 85, Moen, Truk, FSM 96942.
Tel: (691) 303-2432. Telex: 6845.
   Minibus tours of Moen island as well as boat trips to the other islands of the lagoon. Hotel/airport transfers also catered for.

Truk Land and Sea Tour Services, PO Box 502, Moen, Truk, FSM 96942.
Tel: (691) 303-2629.
   Tours of Moen island, showing sites of historical and scenic interest. Fishing and snorkelling trips also organised.

Several Japanese gun emplacements still remain among the islands of Truk Lagoon, along with storage tanks for oil and water, defunct mines and wrecked vehicles.

INDEX

PICTURE CREDITS: Raymond Day (Truk Lagoon Expeditions) 32, 43, 62, 90, 92, 94, 102, 110, 115, 116, 118, 136; Anne-Sophie and Lionel Pozzoli 4, 28, 58, 61 and front cover, 86, 97, 99, 101, 112, 124 and back cover; Roy Smallpage 31, 35 and front cover inset, 49, 54, 83, 107, 131, 133; Brian Humphreys 37, 41, 80, 157; Herwarth Voigtmann (Planet Earth) 26, 69, 70, 142; Carl Roessler (Planet Earth) 72, 122. Maps and line illustrations by Suzanne Hall.